THE INTELLIGENT INVESTOR'S MIND

The Psychology and Philosophy of Smart Investing

By Eldon Frost

Table of Contents

Part V – Words of Warning

Epilogue

Bibliography

Introduction

It is virtually impossible to overestimate the importance of psychology in investing.

Stock choices are based on the psychology of the individual, which in turn affects the thinking of groups of individuals, the market makers, the newsmakers, and the investing world as a whole – and all that is a mirror reflecting back onto itself. Markets move in waves, based on the ebb and flow of investor confidence, greed and panic.

Yet, almost impossibly, psychology is routinely ignored. Investment decisions are based upon charts and graphs, economics, and mathematical models. Computers churn out algorithms to "guess" investor reactions based on logic.

Meanwhile, in the real world, senior citizens rush to banks to withdraw their money after reading frightening business news stories. Blissful newlyweds take out loans and mortgages they cannot possibly afford. Traders scream with delight or throw tantrums, depending on the day.

The stock market is the greatest psychological experiment in the world. With it, you will discover your most valued personal strengths as well as your greatest personal weaknesses, all measured by results in real dollars.

For many, reading this book will *not* be a comfortable experience. A comfortable experience would indicate that you are merely receiving a new interpretation of what you already believe, and are therefore not learning anything. By its very nature, learning and growing involves discomfort. Or, as put more succinctly by R. Barnett: "A genuine higher education is unsettling; it is not meant to be a cosy experience. It is disturbing because, ultimately, the student comes to see that things could always be other than they are."

The Intelligent Investor's Mind is, by necessity, written in two styles.

The first is the traditional Western style of teaching and philosophy – where ideas are introduced, stated, re-stated, and finally summarized to ensure that nothing was missed. The weakness of the Western method is that it does not take into consideration whether or not the reader is ready to receive the information. Two-year olds cannot ride a bicycle – even if it is demonstrated to them – because they do not possess the motor skills to do so. Similarly, information received prematurely is either unrecognizably distorted or inaccurately implemented. The solution to such cognitive distortion is the Eastern method.

The Eastern method of philosophy is to explain by working around the truth, never revealing it or touching it directly. The Eastern method employs simplicity, imparting wisdom by teaching everything except that which is to be learned. Repetition is used to draw emphasis to things that should be emphasized, to purposely introduce mental confusion, and to establish rhythm.

Western readers may initially find the Eastern method perplexing, since they are accustomed to being told the answers, rather than being guided toward them. In some instances, the primary purpose of a section may merely be to prepare one for a revelation later on.

Regrettably, most readers will not look beyond the obvious. Yet, if one is ready, distortions will be peeled away in concentric layers, like an onion, until the truth is finally "revealed" by the gaping void in the middle.

I hope that by the time you finish, you will feel as though a different world has been exposed: that you see clear ideas where others see only chaos; that you can make investment decisions intelligently and without emotion; that you maintain healthy skepticism but without cynicism or fear; and, that you have the personal strength and fortitude to take advantage of what you know.

Beginning Assumptions

You are no doubt reading this book because you desire a shortcut to monetary success (which this is). However, this book makes a very large assumption: it assumes that you have already studied and learned about investing, giving you a basic foundation of knowledge from which to draw upon. This is no small assumption to make.

Most investors plunge in the market long before they have a workable level of knowledge, making themselves their own worst enemies.

On the following pages are 20 questions to determine if you are ready to actively invest in the stock market.

20 Questions

1) If a company goes bankrupt, who is paid first?
   a) Stockholders
   b) Bondholders
   c) Preferred shareholders

2) Which of the following pays the highest dividends?
   a) Common Shares
   b) Corporate Bonds
   c) Government Bonds

3) Which best describes capital gains?
   a) The difference between purchase price and sale price
   b) The total amount of dividends paid
   c) The total amount of interest and dividends paid

4) Which of the following International companies is likely the most cyclical?
   a) ABC Stationary Company
   b) ABC Wire and Steel Company
   c) ABC Breweries Inc.

5) Which of the following investments is least volatile?
   a) High-yield bonds
   b) Long-term bonds
   c) Short-term bonds

6) Which of the following mutual funds has the "best" management expense ratio?
   a) ABC fund, MER of 2.3%
   b) ABC fund, MER of 0.8%
   c) ABC fund, MER of 3.2%

7) Interest rates are climbing. Existing bond prices will
   a) drop
   b) rise
   c) stay the same

8) Which best describes the real rate of return?
   a) The investment rate of return + inflation
   b) The investment rate of return – inflation
   c) The investment rate of return ignoring inflation

9) A Balanced Mutual Fund is best described as
   a) a mix of stocks, bonds, and cash.
   b) A mix of bonds, GICs, and T-bills
   c) A mix of vodka and vermouth with a twist of lemon

10) For an American, investing in Canada or England would primarily represent
   a) political risk
   b) currency risk
   c) depletion risk

11) Investing in a company because the chart looks good is known as
   a) technical analysis
   b) fundamental analysis
   c) Fibonacci swirl analysis

12) All other things being equal, which stock is the best value?
   a) ABC stock, company book value of $1 million with 2 million diluted shares
   b) ABC stock, company book value of $2 million with 2 million diluted shares
   c) ABC stock, company book value of $6 million with 8 million diluted shares

13) All other things being equal, which stock is the most expensive/worst value?
   a) ABC stock, price of $20, EPS of $2
   b) ABC stock, price of $30, EPS of $2
   c) ABC stock, price of $40, EPS of $4

14) For which of the following stocks would a "limit order" be most appropriate?
   a) An international conglomerate company stock
   b) A thinly-traded stock
   c) An exchange-traded fund

15) Market panics usually follow several months of
   a) large-volume, high P/E ratio stock trading
   b) low-volume, low P/E ratio stock trading
   c) low-volume, low interest rate stock trading

16) When a company issues new shares, it typically
   a) is good for existing shareholders
   b) is bad for existing shareholders
   c) has no effect on existing shareholders

17) Net worth or book value is simply defined as
   a) stock price times number of shares
   b) 12-month trailing average stock price
   c) assets minus liabilities

18) A corporate bond investment is best described as
   a) a loan from an individual to a company
   b) an share in the future earnings of a company
   c) an unsecured debt given to a company

19) Stock brokers typically make money
   a) when a client buys a stock
   b) when a client buys or sells a stock
   c) only when a client sells a stock for a profit

20) Which portfolio is likely the least volatile?
   a) Portfolio A – a mix of stocks, bonds, and preferred shares
   b) Portfolio B – a mix of stocks, bonds, and t-bills.
   c) Portfolio C – a mix of stocks, bonds, and debentures

Answer Key:

1)   b
2)   a
3)   a
4)   b
5   c
6)   b
7)   a
8)   b
9)   a
10)   b
11)   a
12)   b
13)   b
14)   b
15)   a
16)   b
17)   c
18)   a
19)   b
20)   b

Score of 16-20 – Pass
Score of 12-15 – Marginal Failure
Less than 12 – Wide Failure

Pass or Fail

If you have passed the test – congratulations! You have a foundation of investment knowledge that will allow you to become a successful investor, provided you do not derail your efforts through psychological weaknesses.

If you did not pass, do not ignore the results, as doing so would constitute your first real failure. The stock market is a zero-sum game: for every buyer there is a seller, and for every winner there is a loser. There are literally thousands of skilled traders and investors ready to take your money. If you invest without basic preparation you will be a lamb in the slaughterhouse.

For the moment, buy a safe (balanced) mutual fund. Then, study diligently until you can pass the test, fully understanding each question. This will require effort.

As a starting point, the author recommends these fundamental readings:

1. "The Intelligent Investor," by Benjamin Graham & David Dodd.
2. "Devil Take the Hindmost," by Edward Chancellor.
3. Any contemporary Series 7 textbook (or CSC in Canada). The Series 7 is the basic test for stockbrokers in the United States.
4. Any contemporary textbook on Macroeconomics (ignore the math; understand the concepts).
5. Any contemporary textbook on Microeconomics.

Part I – Right Reasons & Readiness

Why do you want Success?

If you desire success, and more specifically monetary success, ask yourself: "What is the reason?"

Is it that you want the freedom that comes with money? Perhaps you want to go to a restaurant and order steak and a nice bottle of wine, without worrying about the cost. Maybe you want to take a vacation in the south of France. Is it that you want the stability and safety that money brings? Is it the security of knowing that the modest roof over your head will keep you dry? Perhaps you want money in order to help others, while living modestly yourself. Perhaps you want to acquire money to start a school, or to buy books for those who cannot afford them.

If any of the proceeding reasons are yours, then you may find true success (that is, happiness), provided you don't forget them.

On the other hand, maybe you desire riches in order to "prove yourself." Maybe you have a father, or mother, or uncle, or sister, or brother, or teacher, or neighbor whom you want to impress. Is it that you want to get even? Do you have an enemy, in your mind or in reality, whom you would like to "defeat" through the victory of greater success? Is it that you want power? Perhaps there is someone above you who you would rather see below you. Or, maybe you desire riches for love. Possibly you believe that while there are few who appreciate your affections now, many more might appreciate you if only you had money. Is it because you feel you deserve the best of everything? Perhaps you feel that you should stay in the best hotels, eat the best food, and keep the best company, "because you are worth it."

If any of these are your reasons for desiring monetary success, then forget true success (that is, happiness), because you will find none.

The world has no shortage of "unhappy millionaires," people who continually say, "If only I had more, I would be happy." More could be a faster car, a larger house, a bigger yacht, a more expensive timepiece, a more beautiful spouse – anything.

Unhappy millionaires dedicate their lives to acquiring objects of desire by any means possible and, like anyone who is dedicated, generally end up achieving their goals. In time, they find themselves with sports cars, large houses, yachts and beautiful spouses – exactly as they desired – and are surprised to discover that they are still unhappy. In fact, they are doubly miserable because they cannot understand why they have achieved their goals and yet do not feel complete. Their lives are punctuated by bizarre calamities, as if to remind them of their mortality.

Then there are the "accidental millionaires." These are people who did not necessarily desire extraordinary wealth, but who lived modestly and with reasonable ambition, living ethically because they didn't even consider another way. In time, they find themselves with more wealth than they ever expected, which is icing on the cake for their already complete lives.

There is nothing wrong with wanting luxury, or owning expensive things. But, if you believe that you *require* such things to be happy, you will not remain happy for long. You will always need more. You will never be satisfied.

If you are unhappy living modestly, then you will be equally unhappy living in luxury. Riches will only make your life more complicated and add new responsibilities.

"Nothing satisfies the man who is not satisfied with a little."

Epicurus

Accepting Success

Do you truly desire success?

Most people answer, "Yes," without giving any thought as to whether or not it is true. There are, in fact, many reasons why it is easier to be unsuccessful.

First of all, achieving permanent success requires effort. Many people desire laziness and a high level of permanent success at the same time, which is not possible. Are you willing to put in long hours to achieve success? How about shorter hours but strenuous mental effort? Are you willing to sacrifice your time to study and learn, and keep abreast of developments in your craft? Are you willing to expend your personal energy and direct it toward your goals? In order to gain in one area, you have to sacrifice in another.

Some avoid success because one may derive an equally significant amount of narcissistic supply by easier means. Failing at a business can generate as much sympathy, support, and attention as being successful in the same business, but with far less effort and no planning. Being on the losing end of a stock trade can be as exhilarating as being on the winning end of a stock trade, but with far less effort and no planning.

It is common for a divorced man to say that his wife "ruined him" financially, and forced him to declare bankruptcy. Yet, every year thousands of men get divorced but do not declare bankruptcy. For the prior, bankruptcy is a way of saying to the former spouse, "Do you see what you did to me? Do you see how I am suffering? You should feel guilty!" In this way, post-divorce bankruptcy is a kind of mental revenge, directed against the former spouse. It is also a way of saying to friends and family, "Here is tangible proof of my pain. Please support me." In this way, failure can be a source of comfort.

Those involved in gambling, in abusive relationships, those who live homelessly, who are sexually promiscuous, those with addictions, and those who lose money in the stock market are all, at some level, getting what they want. If they are unable to achieve narcissistic supply from healthier means, they will continue their self-destructive behaviors and have no real desire to stop, even as their inner court beats them up at every turn.

Recognize that depression, sadness and self-pity are all forms of anger; but, since it is impossible to remain angry with ourselves, these are the emotions we feel instead.

If you make a mistake once, it is merely a mistake. If you make this same mistake again, it is foolishness. If you make the same mistake a third time, it is because you want to.

People get what they desire. The difficult part is to get them to realize what they truly desire, and why they desire it.

"The extent to which one realizes one's distance from perfection is the real measure of how successful one may become in Wall Street."

Gerald Loeb

The Tale of Two Brothers

Two brothers, Thomas and Jacob, upon becoming men, began searching for work.

Having come from respectable families, both found jobs easily. Thomas found work as a salesperson, and Jacob found work as a merchant's assistant. However, they soon tired of their jobs.

"I have to coerce people into buying things," lamented Thomas, "and I do not believe in what I am selling. I appreciate my coworkers, but do not find them of the same character as myself." "I also do not like my work," lamented Jacob. "I have to work long hours and holidays. Moreover, people do not appreciate what I do. I want to find a job that I truly love." Both Thomas and Jacob decided to search for new work.

Thomas accepted work as a banker, even though he started in a trivial position. Jacob found work as a jeweler's assistant. After several months, they met to discuss their employers.

"My work as a banker is enjoyable," said Thomas. "Every day I learn something new. I am similar to the people I work with, and the customers appreciate what I do." "That is all well," said Jacob, "but do you love your work? Would you rather work than play?" "No, my work is good," Thomas replied, "but of course I would rather play than work!" "Then, you should look for new work," said Jacob. "You should look for work that you love. And I will do the same."

Jacob began searching for new employment, but Thomas did not heed his brother's advice, instead keeping his job as a banker. After several months, they met to discuss their employers.

"My work as a banker is enjoyable," said Thomas. "Every day I learn something new. I am similar to the people I work with, and the customers appreciate what I do. I am now earning a higher salary, with a better position than before." "That is all well," said Jacob, "but do you love your work? Would you rather work than play?" Thomas replied, "No, my work is good, but of course I would rather play than work!" "Then, you should look for new work," said Jacob. "You should look for work that you love. And I will do the same."

Jacob began searching for new employment, but Thomas did not heed his brother's advice, instead keeping his job as a banker. After several months, they met to discuss their employers.

"My work as a banker is enjoyable," said Thomas. "Every day I learn something new. I am similar to the people I work with, and the customers appreciate what I do. I am now earning a higher salary, with a better position than before." "That is well," said Jacob, "but do you love your work? Would you rather work than play?" Thomas replied, "No, my work is good, but of course I would rather play than work!" "Then, you should look for new work," said Jacob. "You should look for work that you love. And I will do the same."

Jacob continued searching for a job that he would love for the rest of his life.

"The quest for perfection has an element of stupidity to it."

Yo-Yo Ma

The Successful Alchemist

Once upon a time, there lived an old man who had a lovely daughter. She fell in love with a handsome man, and the two soon married. The young couple had a happy life, except that they were always short of money. The young man spent much of his time dreaming of and practicing alchemy – the craft of turning base metals into gold. The young wife scolded her husband for this, but he always said, "We will be rich when I succeed!" The young man indeed worked very hard, reading books about alchemy and practicing his craft from early in the morning until late in the night.

Finally, the young wife told her father about the problem, and he offered to help.

The father visited the young man, and told him that he was working so hard he would surely be successful. "But," the father said, "you are missing the key alchemic ingredient. The ingredient you need is a powder made from the brown star one finds at the bottom of an apple. Many know of it, but few succeed in making gold, since it requires many apples and much effort." The father explained that to make gold requires several pounds of powdered apple stars.

Being ambitious, the young man immediately set about planting apple trees. He cleared land and planted the apple seeds with care. He checked them daily, watered them, picked the weeds and removed the pests. He watched for birds and deer that would eat them. The young man took such good care that soon apple trees grew, with apples from them even when they were mere twigs. At each crop, the young man gave his father-in-law the apples, so that he might take them into town to have the stars removed and ground for powder.

After several years, the young man obtained the necessary powder. "Please show me," he begged his father-in-law, "how to make gold." "I will," the father-in-law replied. "Please come to my house tonight."

Full of excitement, the young man went to the house. When he arrived, the father-in-law laid a small chest upon his lap, and asked him to open it. The young man opened the chest, and was surprised to find it full of gold coins. "In what manner did this gold come?" the young man asked.

"It is yours, from the sale of the apples," his father-in-law replied. "You see. You really have turned base metals into gold."

Five Characteristics of Failure

Much has been written about "winning," or about "the fundamentals of success." Yet, learning about people who have had no success in life can be equally enlightening. Those who lack success share similar characteristics, in the same way as those who have it. Here are five of them. It is your task to see what is shared between these five characteristics, and extrapolate them to discover the hundreds more.

The Variable Locus of Control

Failures take credit for their successes. That is, whenever they find success, they believe it is due to their own actions. Rather than share their good fortune, and attribute successes to the efforts of people who support them, failures typically take the lion's share of the credit. More importantly, though they take credit for their successes, they do not accept responsibility for their shortcomings. Instead of saying, "It was my fault that this happened," they blame others, blame circumstances, blame luck, blame anyone or anything. They do not see how decisions made earlier result in negative outcomes much later. "It's not my fault," and "this would have happened anyway," are the failure's favorite expressions.

Lack of Empathy

Empathy is the ability to understand the circumstances and thoughts of others – commonly described as "the ability to put yourself in the other person's shoes." Lack of empathy leads to selfishness, and selfishness results in a gross lack of ethics and morality.

Undue Pride

Pride in oneself is good. Undue pride, or excessive pride, is believing that one is superior to virtually everyone else. Good advice is therefore disregarded unless it comes from someone "worthy," when in fact good advice can come from anyone. It is far easier for others to spot our weaknesses than for us to spot them in ourselves; but, for someone with undue pride, feedback is wasted because it smashes upon a wall of defensiveness. Undue pride closes the mind, rendering it stagnant and inflexible.

Inability to Delay Gratification

It is easier to eat a seed than to plant one and help it grow. It is easier to play than to study for a college degree. Any great achievement requires the ability to delay gratification. The longer one is willing to delay gratification, the longer one can go without giving up. Planning and patience are the enemies of emotion, and emotion is the enemy of exceptional investing.

Inability to Save

The inability to save is really an inability to delay gratification, but is so important that it warrants its own category. Fear of poverty is an overriding human fear that stands directly in the way of investment success. Saving money regularly, no matter how trivial the amount, gives one the sense of "getting ahead," and reduces the fear of poverty. Money changes emergencies into mere inconveniences. Saving money allows one to take advantage of investment opportunities as they appear.

"If you want to see the greatest threat to your financial future, go home and take a look in the mirror."

Jonathan Clements

The Lost Son – adapted from the tale by Shakyamuni Buddha

There was once a boy, young in years, who abandoned his father, ran away, and lived in another land for fifty years. As he grew older, he found himself unable to obtain the necessities of life, always seeking clothing and food, always wanting.

His father, over those same years, became successful and took up residence in a certain city. His house was full of riches and treasures: gold, lapis lazuli, silver, pearls, ambers and mirrors filled his warehouses. He had servants and attendants, clerks and assistants. Yet, he thought constantly of his son, and his heart was filled with longing and regret.

At this time the impoverished son wandered into the village where his father resided, though he knew this not. He went from house to house, searching for work, until he came to the very house of his father. But when he saw the house filled with diamonds and pearls, rubies and emeralds, gold and silver, he became frightened. He thought to himself: this must be the home of a king, or a man similar to a king, where I might be seized and pressed into service. So he began to run.

At this same moment, the father spotted his son outside the gate and recognized him immediately. His heart was filled with great joy. At once he thought: my son has been in my mind constantly, and now he has appeared.

The father dispatched a messenger, who found the son and made him this offer: he was to come to the rich man's home, and earn double the usual wage, being put to work clearing away excrement. No mention was made that the rich man was his father. The son accepted, and his heart was filled with joy, for he gained that which he did not have before.

The rich man's son worked hard and without complaint, though he was covered in grime and dirt, his clothing in tatters, clearing excrement and filth from the buildings and grounds.

Later the rich man spoke to his son, saying, "You must keep at this work, for you work well. You are not deceitful or lazy, and you do not say resentful or angry words. I will increase your wage and give you salt, rice, vinegar, and the like so you shall not worry. I will be like a father to you." And the rich man assigned a name to the man, as if he were his own child.

The impoverished son was delighted in this treatment, though he still considered himself unworthy and lowly in station. Recognizing this, the rich man kept him clearing away excrement for another twenty years.

At that time the rich man grew ill, and knew that he would die before too long. He spoke to his impoverished son, saying: "I have great quantities of gold, silver, lapis lazuli, and rare treasures which overflow from my warehouses. You are to take charge of what I have, and of what is taken in and given out. You must keep your mind sharp so there are no mistakes or losses."

The impoverished son took over the rich man's finances as instructed, and never thought to appropriate any for himself, even an amount so small as for a single meal. After some time had passed, the son became ashamed of his previously low opinion of himself, and determined to do greater things. Recognizing this change, the father gathered a meeting of noblemen, councilors, ministers and relatives.

When all were gathered together, the father made this announcement: "Gentlemen, you should know that this is my son, who was born to me but lost. His original name is such-and-such, born in the place of such-and-such. For over fifty years he wandered, suffering hardship. Now he has returned to me. Now everything that belongs to me shall belong to him."

When the impoverished son heard these words, he said, "During these last months, I have come to know in my heart that you are my father." His heart was filled with great joy, having gained that which he did not have before. And he thought to himself: I originally had no mind to covet or seek such things. Yet now, they come to me of their own accord.

Part II - Morality and Ethics

Riches without Ethics

Everyone knows of people who are rich and successful – at least by appearances – who got that way despite a substantial lack of ethics, and despite "using" others without remorse or regret. In fact, some believe that the absence of ethics is a *requirement* for extraordinary wealth. In truth, while gold and silver may come via many methods, real wealth (that is, happiness) is not possible if one has become rich by taking from or using others.

There are people who have been led to believe (or who have searched to believe) that there are no such things as universal morals or ethics. "Who can decide what morality is?" they ask. "Who can decide what ethics is?" they ask. They believe that, since views of morality and ethics are dynamic – changing with the age and culture in which we live – they are therefore not tangible and of no real value. They believe that they alone can decide what is moral – a belief that is inevitably self-serving and cold.

Yet, these same people can read a story in a newspaper or hear one from a friend, and say, "Can you believe what happened! Can you believe what this person did! It's terrible!" The story strikes them. They have, without resorting to logic or reason, discovered their own morality. They have pushed this innate sense so far down that they hardly acknowledge it and rarely act upon it; yet, it has never left them.

Others mistakenly believe that they can avoid morality in some areas and still find joy, as long as they compensate by having exceptional morality in other areas. That is, they believe that deep immorality in one area of life is of no consequence, provided that all other areas of one's life are "clean." Still others believe that a life of immorality can be erased by charity – that saving wealth to give away will make life complete, even if that wealth was gained by unethical or immoral means.

Yet, history shows that humanity in one area of life cannot erase inhumanity in another, and that no amount of charitable giving – not even billions of dollars – is enough to atone.

If you try hard enough, you can justify anything that you know is wrong; but myriads of businesspersons, actors, lottery winners and politicians attest to the fact that even with money, lives fall apart without ethical glue. Lasting happiness demands that one sincerely believes, at all levels, that one *deserves* to be happy: this is simply not possible if one leads a selfish, immoral life.

"The death of a daughter is tragic enough, but on top of that, if you are not able to be there – even though you are so rich and powerful – then what does all that power and money mean?"

Isaac Querub, coming to a realization about billionaire oil trader Marc Rich, who was unable to travel from Switzerland to the U.S. to visit his terminally ill daughter due to charges including fraud, racketeering, and tax evasion.

The Life of Jesse Livermore

Jesse Lauriston Livermore was born in 1877, the son of a farmer. Ambitious at a young age, Livermore moved to Boston and got a job as a "board boy," updating stock prices on a chalkboard. From this work, he began to recognize movements in stock prices (Livermore never used charts), and learned to trade. Still in his teens, Livermore made a name for himself as an exceptional stock trader.

Jesse Livermore made most of his money by short selling; that is, by profiting when stock prices drop. Livermore became famous after the Panic of 1907, from which he made over 3 million dollars – an enormous sum in those days. But, in the following years he lost money in bad trade after bad trade, until he declared bankruptcy. He borrowed money to begin anew, and became a millionaire again following the crash of 1929. Once more he lost it all and declared bankruptcy. While he lived, Livermore went from bankrupt to millionaire and back again, several times.

During the prosperous times, Jesse Livermore owned mansions around the world, fleets of Rolls Royce limousines, and luxurious yachts. Personal chefs and servants catered to his every need.

Livermore was a notorious womanizer, having a succession of beautiful mistresses. He married and divorced several times. His second wife, a showgirl named Dorothy, became his bride when she was 18 and he was 41. After she divorced him and took their children, he replaced her with the beautiful Harriet Mentz, despite knowing that her previous four husbands had all committed suicide.

Livermore began drinking heavily. At one point he stumbled into a police station after a long binge, announcing that he had lost his memory.

By the late 1930s Livermore found himself increasingly unable to make money in stocks, due to growing regulations against techniques he had often used, such as front running and market manipulation. Partly to shore up his finances, Livermore wrote a book about his trading secrets, appropriately entitled "*How to Trade in Stocks*," but it did not sell as well as he had hoped.

In a Manhattan hotel, in November of 1940, Jesse Livermore pulled out a .38 caliber revolver and shot himself in the head. In the final entry of his personal notebook, he describes his life as "a failure."

Today, Jesse Livermore is celebrated as one of the most successful stock traders of all time.

Some people work under the assumption that if it isn't illegal, it must be ethical.

The Story of "Pretty Boy" Floyd

Charles Arthur "Pretty Boy" Floyd (1904-1934) was an American bank robber.

Charles Floyd was born into a poor family in the small farming community of Akins, Oklahoma. Married at 16, Floyd looked for work but found nothing substantial. At 18, Floyd began stealing, and began his first jail sentence soon afterward. During his three years in jail, Floyd's wife left him.

Upon his release, Floyd started working as a hired gun for bootleggers and gangsters, and spent his leisure hours learning how to use a machine gun.

In time, he built up a circle of like-minded individuals and began robbing banks. Floyd and his accomplices conducted a stunning series of bank robberies (once robbing 14 banks in 3 months), stealing thousands of dollars and killing several people, including police officers.

Like other gangsters of the time, Floyd was known for his generosity, often giving money to friends and the downtrodden. During this era, a large number of farms were being foreclosed upon due to overproduction, low commodity prices, and economic swings. Floyd considered himself a public benefactor. He was, in his mind, helping by stealing money from the greedy banks and giving it back to the farmers who deserved it (as well as some for himself).

In 1933, the Federal Bureau of Investigation (FBI) started tracking Floyd and his accomplices with increased vigor. Floyd moved to the FBI's "Public Enemy #1" ranking after fellow gangster John Dillinger was killed in Chicago.

On October 22, 1934, in an Ohio field, multiple agents cornered Floyd and opened fire, critically wounding him. Floyd tried to pull out his handgun, but agents disarmed him before he had a chance to use it. Looking down upon his bullet-ridden body, legend has it that Floyd asked, "What have I done to deserve this?"

Floyd passed away shortly thereafter. He was just 30 years old.

Floyd's autopsy revealed several previous, partially healed gunshot wounds in addition to his fresh wounds, along with significant bruising – evidence of his violent existence.

It is estimated that 20-40,000 people attended Floyd's funeral in Sallisaw, Oklahoma.

At a superficial level, everyone thinks they are a good person.

John C. Bogle

John (Jack) Bogle (1929-   ) came from a wealthy and somewhat aristocratic family. Jack's father, a dashing and adventurous man, had flown a Sopwith Camel airplane for the Royal Flying Corp in WWI, before the US entered the war. After the stock market crash of 1929, however, Jack's father found himself short of funds. Though a loving and trusting parent, Jack's father had difficulty adjusting to his new financial status, and lacked the determination to hold steady work. Thus, from an early age all three sons – including Jack – had to work to support themselves.

Jack Bogle graduated from high school in New Jersey, voted "best student" and "most likely to succeed." He received a scholarship to attend Princeton University, working as a waiter during the school year and various odd jobs during summer holidays.

In 1956, Bogle married his wife Eve, with whom he still resides. They would have 6 children.

Bogle studied economics at Princeton, writing his senior thesis on a relatively unknown financial instrument called "mutual funds." He sent the completed thesis to several financial institutions as a type of resume, and soon found work at the Philadelphia-based Wellington Fund. The fund's founder, Walter Morgan, became a trusted mentor and father figure to the young Bogle. When he was just 35 years of age, Bogle was called to a meeting, where Morgan told him that he had found his successor.

At the Wellington Fund (later Vanguard Securities), Bogle made significant changes that brought long-lasting prosperity to the firm – all by placing the customer first. In 1975, for example, Bogle formed the world's first low-cost index fund, that allowed small investors to "buy the market" with a small amount of money. In 1977, Bogle introduced a no-load, sales-charge-free marketing system, and strove for low overhead fees. Investors reacted to the changes by flocking to Vanguard with their money.

Over the years, Bogle has written numerous books and articles touting the value of integrity in the financial industry, calling for reductions in fees, and extolling the merits of long-term thinking (as opposed to speculative trading) on the part of investors. By 2010, he had sold more than 500,000 copies of his books.

Bogle has consistently been a thorn in the side of the investment industry (possibly including his own firm) since many in the industry do not share his belief that "fairness to clients" and "maximum profitability" are compatible goals.

As far back as 1960 (at the age of 30), Bogle had experienced heart problems. Over the years he suffered literally dozens of heart attacks, and by 1995 half of his heart tissue was dead. The following year, he underwent a heart transplant to extend his life. With the support of his family and practitioners, and aided by a positive attitude, he eventually went back to playing golf and squash. At a commencement speech at Trinity College in 2010, Bogle said that despite many health complications since the operation, "If you've been given fourteen additional years of life, it doesn't seem to be a good idea to go around bitching."

In 1999, Bogle was given the Woodrow Wilson award from Princeton University, for "distinguished achievement in the nation's service." He has been a board member of many institutions, including the Investment Company Institute, the Independence Standards Board, and the National Constitution Center. Bogle has received honorary doctorate degrees from Princeton University, University of Delaware, University of Rochester, Eastern University, Widener University, Albright College, Pennsylvania State University, Drexel University, and others.

In the 2009 book *Enough*, Bogle admits that despite years of campaigning for reforms, the financial industry (and Western society in general) has changed little: "We focus too much on *things* and not enough on the *intangibles* that make things worthwhile; too much on *success* (a word I've never liked) and not enough on *character*, without which success is meaningless."

Jack Bogle continues to write and give speeches pressing the importance of personal integrity, fairness, professional conduct, and commitment to society. He says that he has, and continues to, enjoy life to the fullest.

"When you look at the world in a narrow way, how narrow it seems!

When you look at it in a mean way, how mean it is!

When you look at it selfishly, how selfish it is!

But when you look at it in a broad, generous, friendly spirit, what wonderful people you find in it."

Horace Rutledge

Daniel Drew – from Cattle to Railroads

Daniel Drew (1797-1879) was a self-made business tycoon and financier.

He started on his path to riches while in his early 20s, by driving cattle from upstate New York to the butchers in New York City. On his way to NYC, Drew would feed the cattle large quantities of salt but not allow them to drink any water. By the time the cattle arrived in NYC they were terribly dehydrated. Just before presenting the cattle to a butcher, he would allow them to drink copious amounts of water, causing them to bloat. Drew then sold the beasts by the pound, reaping huge rewards. The process became known as "watering stock," and was used in later years to describe financial stocks with little real value. The only disadvantage to this method, Drew wrote, was that he had to sell to "a different butcher 'most every trip."

In addition to driving cattle, Drew sold horses – mostly old, decrepit horses – to unsuspecting purchasers. He would, among other tricks, file the horses' teeth to make them look younger, put saddles on them to hide their sores, and pour hot tar down their throats to make them sound "less winded." Drew apparently felt no ethical turmoil about these practices, stating simply that, "any fellow, except he's a natural-born fool, will look out for number one first."

After finishing his career driving cattle, Drew bought a steamboat and entered the passenger steamboat business, where he developed new, ruthless business strategies. For instance, he hired "runners" to go to the docks of rival companies, to warn travelers that their ships were dangerous and would likely explode. He changed fares purposefully and confusingly; for example, by charging a low rate on a certain day (ex. Wednesday) for weeks until business was booming, then purposefully changing it to a rate three times higher. Drew noted that, due to the difficulties of travel at the time, people would rather pay triple the price than pack up all their belongings and go home.

If a new competitor started along his steamboat routes, Drew would give passengers free tickets – or even pay them – until the competitor was forced out. When one competitor and his steamboat, the *Napoleon*, refused to take the hint, Drew arranged for one of his steamboats to "accidentally" ram it until it nearly capsized, giving the passengers "a scare that they didn't forget for a long time."

Seeing the growth of Wall Street and the easy money found there, Drew founded a bank/brokerage firm and began "speckilating" in stocks, particularly railroads. He manipulated the market heavily, driving up the price of a stock until unsuspecting buyers were drawn in, then quickly selling out, leaving the stock to plummet back to earth. He often short-sold the stock to make extra money on the way down.

Drew profited greatly from stock trading during the US Civil War by paying off Army Generals, telegraph operators and politicians to obtain inside information about war events before they were available to the public. Drew noted, however, that he didn't dare try to bribe President Lincoln, since Abraham Lincoln was "an unpractical man, so far as making money went. All he thought about was to save the Union." The war was so profitable for Drew that he expressed regret when it came to an end.

One day, a man nicknamed "California Parker," whose father had accumulated a fortune, came knocking on Drew's door. He knew that Drew owned Erie railway stock, and made him a business proposal. Together, they would buy large quantities of the stock in the open market to drive up the price, making them both wealthier. Drew accepted.

However, as soon as Parker's heavy buying had raised the price sufficiently, Drew secretly unloaded his shares (to Parker) instead of buying more as promised. Parker anxiously visited Drew's office and asked him to buy more stock to support the price, but Drew flatly refused. When the shell-shocked Parker reminded Drew that he had made a promise, Drew explained that the word "promise" was "just a mere word thrown out in casual talk," and should not have been taken seriously.

Without Drew's support the stock plummeted, and Parker and his family were ruined. Drew thought it was a good joke.

After a time, Daniel Drew's arch-enemy, fellow steamboat operator Cornelius "Commodore" Vanderbilt, became tired of Drew's manipulation of Erie railway stock and worked toward ousting him as a director. Fearful of losing his cash cow, Drew visited Vanderbilt's office, begging Vanderbilt to allow him to stay on the Board. Vanderbilt laughed and said, "Drew, you're as crooked as a worm fence. You'd betray me inside of twenty-four hours!" Drew insisted that he would change, and that he would prove to be a reliable business partner if only given another chance. Vanderbilt, being an optimist, agreed to do so.

The day after returning to his role as director, Drew schemed with partners Jim Fisk and Jay Gould to block Vanderbilt's interests. Vanderbilt had been right – Drew had betrayed him in less than twenty-four hours.

Working with Gould and Fisk, Drew printed 100,000 shares of new Erie stock to water down Vanderbilt's shares, destroying their value. Vanderbilt wasted millions trying to support the stock price as Drew secretly pumped out the newly printed shares. Yet, Vanderbilt would have the last laugh. The following day, a messenger arrived to tell the trio that there was a warrant out for their arrests, for the illegal printing of shares.

The three fled across the state line to Jersey City, where they holed up in a hotel. Drew was so terrified of being abducted by bounty hunters that he hired a small army to protect the hotel, including fifteen police officers and a force of Erie rail employees complete with cannons.

Finally, after a month of exile, Drew met with Vanderbilt and brokered a deal – Vanderbilt would allow Drew to return to New York if Drew bought back all the newly issued stock. Drew wrote that he learned never to mess with a man as powerful as himself.

As treasurer of the Erie railroad, Drew was blamed for allowing the rails to wear down without replacement (so that he could use the money to speculate in the stock market), resulting in a crash that killed twenty-two passengers, some of them burned alive. The press called it "murder." In his diary, Drew admits that, on several occasions, he used the money intended for new rails for personal use, but states that he felt "entitled to it."

Drew was a man greatly proud of his wealth, believing that it proved he was better than other men. He also believed that having money compensated for his lack of education: "book learning is something," he wrote, "but thirteen million dollars is also something, and a mighty sight more." Finally, he believed (often rightly) that money gave him both power and legal impunity.

A self-professed devout Christian, Drew lost and rediscovered religion several times in his life. His philosophy was that ethics in business and in home life were two completely separate things, and (conveniently) believed that God didn't judge a person by the business side. In fact, he worried about the souls of his womanizing business partners, considered them morally corrupt, and thought it his duty to try to "save" them.

As a dedicated philanthropist, Drew built the Daniel Drew church, the Drew Ladies' Seminary, and the Drew Theological Seminary (that later became Drew University). He believed that faith was an "all cleansing fountain" that absolved one of all sins, even if those sins were ongoing. He once boasted that "some of the people" started calling Daniel Drew church the "Saint Daniel Drew church."

In 1868, Drew and his business partners, Fisk and Gould, devised a new scheme to short-sell stocks and increase their fortunes. They went to several banks, and demanded back all their deposits in cash (millions of dollars worth), on the same day. They knew that in order to get the cash, the banks would have to call in their loans. One bank manager warned Drew that making the withdrawals would cause great hardship to great numbers of people, to which Drew replied, "I'm not in business for the benefit of your other depositors and clients."

The result was financial panic. The stock market sank, multi-generational businesses went bankrupt overnight, and farmers lost their lands. Drew, fearing that he might be murdered by angry citizens, gave his money back to the banks to wash his hands clean of the deal, angering Fisk and Gould in the process. "I hadn't thought the thing would kick up such a rumpus," Drew wrote. As usual, he avoided lawsuits by paying off judges. When a newspaper writer wrote an article criticizing the trio for their actions, he had the writer arrested.

In 1869, Drew heard a sermon about making God your business partner. He spent the night praying, then went down to the stock exchange in the morning and began buying Erie stock. He didn't know that while he was selling Erie stock short, Fisk and Gould were going long. The trade heavily damaged Drew's finances. When Drew went to ask Fisk for an extension to pay, his old partner replied, "Look happy, Uncle, look happy. Of course we shall be under the necessity of taking nearly all of your earthly possessions. But there are other things in life besides money." Drew was furious but soon got over it, since Drew himself believed that men with a conscience have no place in business.

In the following months and years, Drew continued to lose money through a succession of bad trades, general market panics (some of which he was responsible for starting), and failed business ventures. Drew and Gould backstabbed each other on several occasions, each time pretending to forgive the other and become friends. Facing angry creditors, Drew told everyone he was ill and began to avoid public appearances.

Finally, in 1876, Daniel Drew filed for bankruptcy. He had gone from being one of the richest men in the history of America to personal bankruptcy in just under six years.

Drew's initial plan was to move back to his home county of Putnam and spend the rest of his life living modestly and peaceably. However, he soon found himself being harassed for payments by farmers he had swindled years earlier, in his cattle droving days. He decided to move back to New York.

In New York, Drew tried to regain his position as a market player but found, to his astonishment, that no one wanted to deal with him. He began spending whole days in bed, feeling too weak to leave home and too depressed to receive visitors. He also began suffering from "epileptic attacks" (possibly panic attacks).

Drew installed a stock ticker in the rented home he shared with his son, never giving up on the idea of making "a lucky hit" and regaining his former glory. It never came. Until his death in 1879, Drew was dependent upon his son for daily living expenses.

Of Drew's business partners, Jim Fisk was shot and killed at age 37 by a rival of his mistress. Senator Bill Tweed (whom the trio often bribed) went to jail for political corruption, where he remained until his death. Jay Gould, the most educated of the three, retained his monetary wealth and lived lavishly, though he reportedly remained "lonely and troubled" after Fisk's death. Gould died at age 56 after two years of nervous breakdowns. Gould's son Howard committed suicide at the age of 21.

Most of Daniel Drew's business practices are now illegal.

"…the old fashioned theory (as some people call it) about guilt bringing with it its own punishment, receives a startling illustration in the events of the past year…The men of whom Fisk was one seemed to be so strong that nothing could shake them. They had wealth and power unlimited; they altered laws to suit themselves; leaders of society bowed down before them. The world had nothing more to offer them. But to the astonishment of all men, as if it were in a moment, a whirlwind descends upon them, and they are swept away."

The New York Times, Jan 7th, 1872: the day after the death of James (Jim) Fisk.

John Templeton

John Templeton was born in Winchester, Tennessee in 1912.

In high school, the highly industrious Templeton taught himself – and his classmates – the math studies that the school was unable to provide. After graduation, he was accepted to Yale University.

Templeton's father, despite being a lawyer, was hit hard by the Great Depression and was unable to keep paying his son's fees for Yale. Not willing to give up, Templeton started doing work for the university and also gambling at poker, which, with his propensity for numbers, often put him on the winning side.

Having successfully completed his studies at Yale, he got a Rhodes scholarship and finished his studies at Oxford, earning a Masters Degree in Law. Templeton said that the wealthy schools of Yale and Oxford were where he first learned what rich investor's personalities were like, and what they wanted.

After Oxford, Templeton and a college friend spent seven months touring 35 countries, on a budget of less than a dollar a day. They slept on ship's decks, ate stale bread and fruit from trees, and had a spectacular time. This experience in thrift, he later said, was good for him.

Before leaving for his travels, Templeton had written letters to 100 investment firms, telling them that he would be available for hire when he got back. Upon his return in 1937, he found a job waiting for him at an investment firm in New York. That same year, he married his first wife, Judith Folk. Judith would die in a motorcycle accident fourteen years later, after giving him three children.

Templeton did well in the investing world due to his disciplined and contrarian views. In 1939, for instance, Hitler invaded Europe and markets crashed. Templeton, believing that stocks were undervalued, bought 100 shares each of 104 companies, all of which were selling for less than a dollar. All but three resulted in huge profits.

In 1940, he bought a small investment firm. The firm did reasonably well until 1954, when Templeton established a new mutual fund in Canada. At that time Canada had no capital gains tax, and the Templeton Growth Fund was born. From 1954 to 1992, the fund grew by 14.5% a year: a $10,000 investment would have grown to $2,000,000.

Loyal investors thronged to the Templeton Fund's annual meetings, where Templeton dispensed tidbits of investing wisdom, as well as his market predictions for the coming year.

Templeton remarried in 1958 to Irene Reynolds Butler, with whom he had a daughter. She would pass away in 1993 after 35 years of marriage.

Templeton moved to the Bahamas in 1968, a move that he was criticized for (mostly by the US Government, who said he was avoiding taxes). Templeton himself admitted that taxation was part of the reason, but added that living far away from Wall Street was good for making sound investment decisions (a reasoning shared by billionaire Warren Buffett, who chose to remain living in Omaha, Nebraska). The fine weather was likely another factor.

Templeton lived well. His estate in the Bahamas had an ocean view, with orange trees and an abundance of flowers. Visitors to the estate were treated royally, with British-style breaks for afternoon tea.

Aside from his estate, however, Templeton was said to have been "uninterested" in consumerism, driving his own car, and not caring about luxury goods or flashy shows of wealth. A nephew recalled that even after they were wealthy, the family went traveling across Europe in a Volkswagen bus, eating bread and cheese and staying in modest accommodations (Templeton's idea was to teach the children the benefits of frugality: a budget was set, and the children got to keep whatever money remained after the trip. The children almost immediately stopped wanting to eat at fancy restaurants).

Templeton was involved in philanthropic activities throughout his life. He created the "Templeton Prize" in 1972, the winner being judged on philosophy, exemplary conduct, creativity, and other attributes. In 1984 he endowed Templeton College, a business and management school at Oxford. In 1987, the same year he created the Templeton Foundation, Queen Elizabeth II knighted him. Templeton also used his time to write several books.

With regard to spirituality and his Templeton Prize, he said: "I grew up as a Presbyterian. Presbyterians thought the Methodists were wrong. Catholics thought all Protestants were wrong. The Jews thought the Christians were wrong. So, what I'm financing is humility. I want people to realize that you shouldn't think you know it all." Templeton shocked some Christians when he said that he would attend Hindu or Muslim services, if he chose, so that he could "learn more."

In 1992, Templeton sold the Templeton family of funds, from which he personally received $440 million. His net worth later grew into the billions.

John Templeton died of pneumonia at the age of 95, in the Bahamas.

"To continue much longer overwhelmed by business cares and with most of my thoughts wholly upon the way to make more money in the shortest time, must degrade me beyond hope of permanent recovery."

Andrew Carnegie, Age 33

The Life of J. Paul Getty

J. Paul Getty was the son of a successful American oil field developer. By age 23, Getty had made his first million dollars, and retired to live as a playboy in California. However, he presumably tired of this lifestyle, since he returned to business only a few years later. Getty's father was purportedly aghast at his son's antics.

After the stock market crash of 1929, Getty wisely made acquisitions of other oil companies at reduced prices, and merged them into Getty Oil.

From research, Getty became convinced that oil existed in a place called Saudi Arabia, though none had yet been found there. After years of drilling and investigation, Getty discovered one of the richest oil fields in the world.

During his life, Getty was married and divorced five times (often getting remarried in the same year as his divorce), and was known for taking lovers. He had six sons with four of his wives.

Always popular in high society, for most of his life Getty hobnobbed with Presidents, sheiks, royalty, and movie stars.

Getty's youngest son, George, died of a lethal combination of alcohol and barbiturates. Getty's eldest son, Timothy, survived several brain tumor operations, only to die after what was supposed to have been a minor cosmetic surgery: he was 12.

In 1976, Getty's grandson, John Paul Getty III, was kidnapped in Italy. Believing that paying the ransom would incite more of the same, Getty refused payment until his grandson's ear was finally sent to him in an envelope. Initially the kidnappers wanted $3.2 million USD, but Getty negotiated with them until he had reduced the sum to $2 million. Getty loaned his son (the father of the child) the ransom money, and made him repay it at 4% interest.

J. Paul Getty lived his final years at his palatial Sutton Place estate in England, protected by an elaborate electronic surveillance system, a security force and guard dogs. He died of heart failure at the age of 83.

As his philanthropic legacy, he left behind the J. Paul Getty museum, the Getty foundation, the Getty Research Institute, and the Getty Conservation Institute, with almost $700 million going to the museum alone upon his death.

"There is a Law of Compensation in Nature. Every plus is somewhere, somehow offset by a minus."

J. Paul Getty

Two Parrots

There were once two parrots, one large and one small, with beautiful feathers of red, yellow and green. Their eyes glistened with the joys of life, and their grips were strong.

The two parrots lived in a fig tree, which they loved dearly. They loved the way its green leaves protected them from the heat of the sun, and from the dampness of the rain. They loved the way it swayed gently in the breeze, and the way the wind whistled through its branches. They loved eating the sweet figs that grew so abundantly. The parrots felt content living in the fig tree. "We will never leave you," the parrots said to the tree, "because you have been so good to us."

The gods watched these birds from the heavens, and wondered about their strength of character. "Do they deserve to be so happy?" the gods wondered.

The gods made the fig tree's leaves wither and dry, until they began falling to the ground. Soon, the tree was bare. Dust gathered on the branches when the weather was dry, and raindrops pelted the birds when the weather was wet. The figs grew stale. Finally, the large parrot could take no more.

"I will find another tree," the large parrot said, "as this one's usefulness has passed." With that, it flew away. But the second parrot did not leave. "Friends do not part, merely because of a change in fortune," the small parrot said to the tree. "I will stay with you."

The large parrot soon found another tree, with green leaves that protected it from the heat of the sun, and from the dampness of the rain. The tree swayed gently in the breeze, and the wind whistled through its branches. Figs grew abundantly. Yet despite its easy life, the large parrot was frequently struck with melancholy and regret.

Hours became days, days became weeks, weeks became months, but still the small parrot stayed with the tree, watching the sun rise and set. "I will stay with you," he said to the tree, never wavering.

The gods looked down upon the small parrot, and were well satisfied. "Little bird," they said, "you have a loyal and faithful heart."

Despite its hardships, the small parrot lived contentedly for the rest of its days.

Virtue and Excellence – A Conclusion

In 399 BC, the philosopher Socrates wrote: "I tell you that virtue is not given by money, but that from virtue comes money and every other good of man, public as well as private." Unfortunately, this is not entirely true.

The acquisition of money also requires effort, diligence, sound judgment, and the ability to recognize and take advantage of opportunities as they present themselves. Not to be misunderstood, "opportunity" does not refer to any situation that can make one money, give one pleasure, or advance one's interests. A real opportunity does these things, but does so upon a principled foundation. An "opportunity" which lacks a principled foundation is no opportunity at all.

The universe is never entirely fair, for it is a chaotic place. Good people contract terminal diseases, are involved in tragic accidents, and suffer great hardships; those devoid of moral and ethical sense, however, seem to receive far more than their share. More importantly, those devoid of moral and ethical sense find few people there to support them when they do.

To ignore one's innate sense of rightness, or to slay it using perverse logic, is to invite peril and misery. Likewise, those waiting to change or to make good, always wait too long.

"Believe me, my young friends, the best and surest guard against the inconveniences of old age, is to cultivate in each preceding period the principles of moral science, and uniformly to exercise those virtues it prescribes. The good seeds which you shall thus have sown in the former seasons of life will, in the winter of your days, be wonderfully productive of the noblest and most valuable fruit – valuable not only as a possession which will remain with you even to your latest moments, but also as a conscious retrospect on a long life marked with an uninterrupted series of laudable and beneficent actions affords a perpetual source of the sweetest and most exquisite satisfaction."

Cicero, *Cato Maior de Senectute*
(An Essay on Old Age), 44 BC

Part III – Logical Thinking

The Truth is Never the Truth

In the past people believed, with certainty, that the earth was at the center of the universe, that life spontaneously generated from mud, that moodiness was caused by an excess of bile, that witches rode brooms and sailed the seas in eggshells, that the stomach was the seat of emotion, that female insanity was caused by an overactive uterus, and that the mind and body are separate. Importantly, these things were all believed well after the discovery of the scientific method.

In a hundred years much of what we believe today will be regarded as nonsense. All of our ideas, thoughts and feelings are interpreted through the filter of beliefs that we hold at this time, commonly known as our zeitgeist (time ghost). When someone coughs, we say they have a cold (virus), not an imbalance of humors. When someone screams and curses in public for seemingly no reason, we determine that they are mentally ill, not that they are possessed by the devil. Our way of thinking is not only a snapshot of the time we live, but also of the culture that we grew up in. Even the most basic and irrefutable of truths today will change.

"Quid est Veritas?" – What is Truth?

Pontius Pilate

Three Blind Men and the Elephant

Three blind men were gossiping one day, when one of them said, "I heard that the elephant is an amazing creature. It is too bad that we are blind and unable to see one." "Yes," said the second blind man, "but maybe we can feel one, which will give us an idea what the animal is like." "An excellent idea!" said the third blind man.

The three blind men found a merchant with an elephant, who agreed to let them visit it. The merchant led the three men to his elephant and said, "Elephants are shy, and so I will take you one at a time to touch it." All agreed.

The first blind man was led to the rear of the elephant. He touched the tail, which was swishing back and forth. "Truly a strange animal," the blind man said. "Now I know what an elephant is like."

The second blind man was led to the side of the elephant, where he touched the legs. "It is like a man, standing on tree trunks," he said.

The third blind man was led to the front of the elephant, where he touched the trunk. "It is like a large snake, with prickly hair!" he said.

After the merchant left with his elephant, the three men agreed to discuss what they had discovered.

"The elephant is wispy and thin, not at all what I expected," the first blind man said. "What!" exclaimed the second blind man, "it is tall and thick, like a pair of trees!" "No!" the third man exclaimed, "it is like a large snake!"

The three men spent the rest of the day arguing, each insisting that he alone was correct.

They remained blind forever.

"Approval…is not the goal of investing. In fact, approval is often counter-productive because it sedates the brain and makes it less receptive to new facts or a re-examination of conclusions formed earlier."

Warren Buffett

Reverse Attribution

Investors should be aware that the market is understood via "reverse attribution" (also known as "*post hoc ergo propter hoc*"). That is, after a market event has occurred, analysts try to determine why it happened and report it as news. The results are, predictably, often overly simplistic or simply wrong.

In 1929, trader Jesse Livermore sensed a change in the public. After months of positive news, he sensed that people were getting bored with the "prosperity" story. Livermore knew that a well-known economist, Roger Babson, was going to give a speech the following day, saying that markets were overpriced and due for a crash. Livermore knew that this would be Babson's speech because it was the same speech that Babson had given the previous two years.

Recognizing the opportunity, Livermore sold short vast quantities of stock (meaning that he would make a profit if the market declined), and then had his staff of secretaries call every major news agency in the U.S. and alert them to an "important speech" that was about to take place. When Babson's press conference occurred, it was to a packed crowd of eager reporters.

The following day, Babson's dire predictions made front-page headlines, and the market took a frightening dive. This was the beginning of the end for investor confidence in 1929. The infamous "Great Crash" occurred less than two months later, with many blaming Livermore's orchestrated press conference as the catalyst that started it.

A few years ago, a mutual fund manager related the story of when his fund decided to sell a large quantity of a certain company's stock. The day they started selling just happened to coincide with an announcement by the company, saying that they were changing some of their board members.

The next days' headline: "*X* company stock drops after appointment of new board members – investors not pleased with changes."

In the book *Wall Street Meat*, Andy Kessler tells the story of a German banker who decided to have some fun at the annual Christmas party. The inebriated banker called in an order to buy a massive number of shares in a pharmaceutical company.

As the whole party watched the viewing screen in anticipation, the share price ticked higher and higher due to the onslaught from the huge order. When the newswire reported "heavy buying" by a foreign investor, the partygoers screamed with delight. Finally, the New York Stock Exchange halted the buying on rumors that this was a takeover attempt.

Disappointed that the fun was over, the partygoers went back to their steins and punchbowls to continue their Christmas celebration. The following morning the large purchase was quietly sold off.

When news agencies have no idea why markets are moving, they employ common expressions; most notably, "profit taking" (to describe a drop) and "bargain hunting" (to describe a gain). For instance, "the markets went up today on bargain hunting," is a convenient way to explain an increase in the market on a day with no substantial news.

On any given day, no one knows precisely why stocks move. Sometimes guesses are, for the most part, accurate. Sometimes they are dead wrong. Sometimes they cite a single reason when in fact there are many. It's up to you to dig further. It's up to you to know that sometimes people manipulate the market for fun or for personal gain.

"It is customary to refer with great respect to the 'bloodless verdict of the marketplace,' as though it represented invariably the composite judgement of countless shrewd, informed and calculating minds. Very frequently, however, these appraisals are based on mob psychology, on faulty reasoning, and on the most superficial examination of inadequate information."

Benjamin Graham

Cognitive Dissonance

"Cognitive dissonance" is the name for anxiety caused by disconcerting thought processes. That is, when people are faced with facts that make them uncomfortable, they tend to ignore these facts, literally to the point of self-denial.

Cognitive dissonance is the reason why a mother won't accept that her son is dead, even when the police are standing in the doorway telling her. Cognitive dissonance is the reason why a husband with an unfaithful wife will always be the last to know. It is why those in debt do not open their mail. It is why gangster Al Capone believed he was a good person because he donated to charity. And, it is why Americans who bought real estate in 2006 insisted that there was no bubble, despite all evidence to the contrary.

It is natural for people to seek confirmation of their existing beliefs. Finding facts to prove you are right is both satisfying and comfortable. But in order to be a truly effective thinker, one must embrace cognitive dissonance by intentionally seeking disconfirming evidence. The greatest discoveries in history have come from people who refused to blindly accept the flawed "truths" of their day. And, one of the best techniques for embracing cognitive dissonance is a simple one known as "inversion."

Inversion states that you should take every question or idea that you have, and examine it as if you had the opposite belief. Stated another way, for any strong belief that you have, you should intentionally and regularly search for evidence you might be wrong; or, alternatively, look for reasons why you can't be right.

If you wish to buy a stock, for example, you would include a search for reasons *not* to buy it. You would read not just the glowing press releases about the company, but also seek out all negative facts about the company, and judge these facts without emotion. Only after finding no significant reasons *not* to buy the stock would you actually buy it.

To find truth, you must embrace cognitive dissonance. You must embrace the fact that many of your existing beliefs are wrong, and therefore constantly challenge them.

Cognitive dissonance is not easy to overcome. You will be fighting natural human emotion every step of the way. But, by making a habit of questioning your own judgments and attempting to prove your own beliefs false, you will become a stronger and more reliable investor (and possibly a better person). Soon, you will find your mental discomfort becoming a source of pride and pleasure – not to mention lucrative.

"Faced with the choice between changing one's mind and proving there is no need to do so, almost everyone gets busy on the proof."

John Kenneth Galbraith

The Rice Farmer

A rice farmer named Koji reasoned that although his profits were good, they would be much better if he were able to plant three crops a year instead of the usual two. All he would need to do, he reasoned, would be to plant his rice at the earliest possible moment in the season.

One day, in the middle of the first month of the year, the sun broke out with a warm glow, and the sky turned deep blue. This was the type of weather perfect for growing rice! The following day, Koji awoke to find another warm and beautiful day. The following day was more beautiful still.

Koji flooded his rice paddies and began planting. The very next day, a cold breeze blew in from the north and the sky clouded over. That night, all of his rice fields froze.

Koji lamented his loss. "I should have known," he said, 'that a warm day in January does not mean that spring has arrived."

"It seems that the immature mind has a regrettable tendency to believe, as actually true, that which it only hopes to be true."

Fred Schwed, Jr.

The Piltdown Man Hoax

The Bible says that God created man in his image. So, when Charles Darwin suggested that humans evolved from ape-like creatures, the religious community saw it as blasphemous. Darwin was ridiculed for his radical beliefs.

At the same time, a small but growing group of scientists and non-believers embraced what they saw as Darwin's sensible ideas. These scientists, longing for an alternative to Biblical creation, traveled the globe searching for evidence of evolution. At first, such evidence was not forthcoming.

The search for the "missing link" (the ancestor of modern humans) became so powerful that – not wanting to wait for real evidence – one man simply manufactured it.

In 1912, Charles Dawson announced that he had found the proverbial missing link in a gravel pit in England. Though Piltdown man's authenticity was contentious from the beginning, it was not until 1953 that it was conclusively exposed as a fraud, when it was proven that "Piltdown man" was in fact a human skull combined with the jawbone of an orangutan.

The Piltdown man hoax resulted from men trying to prove their existing beliefs true, even though good science necessarily does the opposite.

It has been over a hundred years since Darwin first proposed the theory of evolution, and people's interpretations of it have evolved dramatically since then (pun intended).

The first "modern" biology textbook, incorporating evolution, was written by George W. Hunter and published in 1914. It states that there are five races of man: the Ethiopian or negro type; the Malay or brown race; the American Indian; the Mongolian or yellow race and – "the highest type of all" – the Caucasian or white race. The textbook explains that diseases such as tuberculosis and syphilis are genetic, and suggests that those who have such diseases should not be allowed to reproduce. It also describes "parasitic" peoples who take from society but give nothing in return. Such references were gradually removed from high school textbooks following World War II.

The theory of evolution – in its current form – is well recognized and accepted not only in the scientific community, but also as part of the collective zeitgeist. Dating, sex, sports, politics, family life, business, careers, music and more are now analyzed and understood through the filter of evolution.

In light of the overwhelming evidence in support of evolution, scientists today who reject the theory are often ridiculed.

"All truth passes through three stages. First, it is ridiculed. Second, it is violently opposed. Third, it is accepted as being self-evident."

Arthur Schopenhauer

Investment Reasoning – Logical Fallacies

       Logical Fallacies are, quite simply, flaws in reasoning. The stock market and its participants are plagued with flawed reasoning, yet few (except the best) are even aware of it. Every day, so-called professionals can be seen giving their opinions in completely illogical and faulty arguments, while fellow investors nod in agreement.

       Following are the most prevalent logical fallacies found in regard to the stock market. Learning to recognize them (that is, learning to ignore them and to reason accurately) puts you ahead of the crowd. Note that these fallacies are not exclusive – they overlap – and a single statement may include several.

Irrelevant Conclusion (the "Red Herring") – A statement of questionable relationship to the argument, which does not address the original issue (often meant to draw attention away from the argument).

Example: "The economy isn't doing well. Bob's shoe store is really slow."
Example: "If you drink beer, you will die young."

Ad hominem **(Reduction to Humanity)** – A statement that disregards a conclusion by attacking the person making it.

Example: "She's been wrong so much, she can't possibly be right about this."
Example: "The government is corrupt. The Federal Reserve must be lying."

Implying Causation from Correlation – Implying that something is the direct cause of another, when there may only be a relationship.

Example: "Large cities in the United States have more police officers than small cities. Large cities have more crime than small cities. The police must be criminals."
Example: "He must be a great investor because he's rich."

Note that this fallacy has a tendency to be abused, by using it to disregard all correlations, no matter how relevant. For example, in the 1980s, tobacco companies disregarded all studies linking smoking to lung cancer.

Probability Appeal – Assuming that because something *could* happen, it is inevitable that it *will* happen.

Example: "Gold could hit $9000 an ounce. Therefore, you should buy gold."
Example: "Stay away from banks. The US financials index may go to zero."

False Dichotomy – Falsely reducing a set of many possibilities to only two choices.

Example: "The forecast says it will not rain tomorrow, so it should be sunny."
Example: "The market can't keep expanding at this pace. Within weeks it will fall."

Fundamental Attribution Error – The tendency for people to over-emphasize personality-based explanations for behaviors observed in others, while under-emphasizing situational influences on the same behavior.

Example: "That CEO is terrible. Just months after he joined the company, the stock dropped."
Example: "This stock analyst is great! Every stock she recommended has gone up!" (said in a rising market).

Gambler's Fallacy – Assumes that the outcome of a random event is influenced by previous outcomes.

Example: "The last four roulette wheel spins have been black. The next one will be red for sure."
Example: "The last time the market hit x level, it jumped 20 points. So, it should do so again."

Information Bias – The tendency to seek information beyond what is useful, leading to less accurate decisions.

Example: "Judith is an expert on Coca-Cola® stock. She knows the seasonality of Coke® sales for each country, and the production capacity of each plant."

Endowment Effect (The "Puppy Dog" Effect) – The tendency for people to demand much more to give up an object than they would to acquire it.

Example: "I love this antique vase. I bought it for $500 last week, but I wouldn't sell it for less than $900" (the person would not have spent $900 to acquire it).

Example: "I paid $30 per share, so I won't sell it for less than $30" (said even when the company's business fundamentals are deteriorating).

Anchoring – The tendency for people to attach themselves to a reference point, whether or not that reference point is relevant to the decision being made.

Example: "I got a great deal on this watch! The salesperson was asking $400, but I bargained him down to $200" (the actual retail price was $80).
Example: "This stock is cheap! It used to be $50 but now it's only $10" (said about a company near bankruptcy, with little hope of recovery).

Clustering Illusion – The strong tendency to see patterns where none exist.

Example: "When skirts are short, the stock market always crashes."
Example: "This stock is channeling in a broadening reverse symmetrical pattern, so major price changes in the near future are unlikely."

Overconfidence Effect / Illusory Superiority – The tendency for people to overestimate their abilities.

Example: "I know that real estate is overpriced, but I will see the selloff coming and get out before anyone else."
Example: "I'm a better investor than most people" (said by the majority of investors).

If you call a "tail" a "leg," how many legs does a dog have?

Answer: 4

Intellectual and Social Readiness

Galileo proposed that the sun, not the earth, was the center of the universe, and for this belief he spent much of his life under arrest. William Harvey was ostracized for his belief that the blood circulates in the body. Louis Pasteur was criticized for believing that the air contains living organisms.

Be aware that if you tell people the truth, and the intellectual climate of the time is not ready to accept it, your ideas will not only be rejected but will be vigorously denied. In fact, the greater the originality of a new truth, the more it will be resented.

People naturally enjoy familiarity, search for patterns, and invent details or make interpretations based upon experience (or just wishful thinking). An argument that seems logical on the surface may involve no logic at all. Though such cognitive shortcuts serve us well on a day-to-day basis, they can also be destructive.

Fortunately, for investors the stock market is a fair judge and jury. Within a few years (and sometimes within a few minutes), it rewards those whose beliefs are right, and punishes those whose beliefs are wrong.

Part IV – How to Invest

What is a Stock?

A common share, or stock, is part ownership of a company. If a company has a total value of $10 million, with 1 million shares, then each share is, technically, worth $10. Owning a share means that one owns 1/1,000,000th of every chair, desk, building, and pen that belongs to that company. It also means that the shareholder owns 1/1,000,000th of all the future earning potential of the company.

The confusing part about share ownership is that most of the time, the price of a stock has no direct relationship to the value of the company the stock represents. Even in the absence of major news, the price of a stock can go up or down 5 or 10% in a single day, despite the unlikelihood of the company's true value changing so significantly.

There are occasions – usually during times of extreme cynicism – where, for example, a company can have $10 worth of cash per share, yet the stock will be trading in the market at only $8. That is, you can buy $10 cash for $8, and get an entire company thrown in for free.

There are only three instances when a stock tends to accurately represent the intrinsic value of the company: when that company is bought, is sold, or goes into bankruptcy. Other than these cases, the price of a stock represents little more than the whims of investor expectations and moods, which may or may not be realistic.

In the long term, stocks tend to fluctuate around the true value of the company. The goal of a successful investor is to buy a stock when it is undervalued, and sell it when it is overvalued.   That is, to buy when the stock price is clearly lower than the value of the company it represents, and sell it when the stock price is clearly higher than the value of the company it represents.   In practice, this generally means buying unpopular or ignored companies and selling popular ones, or buying great companies during times of fear and selling them during times of euphoria.

Pure speculation, or trading, is different from investing. Trading is the art of anticipating the moods and whims of investors, and buying or selling in response. Because investor psychology is intangible and fleeting, trading is therefore far more difficult than investing. Even experienced traders tend to, after years of successful trading, lose not only their gains but also their initial principle.

Emotion takes a central place in speculation, but has no place in investing.

There are thousands of reasons why a stock may drop:

- A company may miss an analyst's target
- The whole market may drop
- A large shareholder may need to sell stock to buy Christmas presents
- The whole industry may be unpopular
- Another industry might be more popular
- The Federal Reserve may raise interest rates, which is bad for short-term business
- The President of the US might be assassinated
- There could be a terrorist attack
- Sales and revenues of the company may be dropping
- The company may take on too much debt
- and more

Notice that almost all the reasons listed are psychological, and not related to the viability of the company directly. Yet, individual investors routinely mistake a falling stock price for a weak underlying company, or a rising stock price for a strong company.

The Business Cycle – As Experienced by a Retail Investor

What marks the retail investor (the average non-professional) is fear caused by lack of understanding, occasionally accompanied by overconfidence. One goal of investing, then, is to accumulate enough understanding not to be a menace to yourself, while at the same time recognizing your limitations. An important step in this process is to understand how most investors behave, and how this differs from the best. As a rule, retail investors follow a pattern similar to the following scenario…

As the economy begins to recover from a recession, retail investors remain skeptical (or frightened and angry) and stay on the sidelines, putting their money into low-interest guaranteed investments and money market funds, or hidden in their homes. They aren't aware (or don't care) that when inflation is at 3% and their investments yield 2%, they are actually losing money.

As the economy improves and stocks begin to rise, they remain in cash. The market continues to rise, but with occasional drops (corrections) that keep edgy investors out of the market, and leads them to believe that the market is rigged against them. Eventually, after stocks have risen significantly and the economy is well on its way to recovery, news stories of "excellent markets" begin to make headlines. At this point, retail investors begin buying mutual funds and stocks in quantity.

The return of retail money to the market causes stocks to rise. Seeing their stock values improving, retail investors get excited and put even more money into the markets. Markets rise dramatically. Increasingly, stocks become overpriced.

The "fantastic economy" makes front-page news. Friends and neighbors of existing investors, not wanting to miss out on becoming rich, join the party. News reports explain that this economy is different from all others before it (due to the Internet, Globalization, rise of China, or some other justification) and that therefore the good times will never end. Traditional measures of value, like a company's earnings and debt levels, are said to no longer matter: any price is justified.

Consumers, flush with cash and psychologically uncomfortable with their new level of wealth, look to rid themselves of it as quickly as possible. The resulting spending spree causes wage increases, labor shortages and inflation. Young workers skip work to go to the beach, confident that if they get fired they will be able to find a new job within days.

The Federal Reserve begins to warn the public using cryptic phrases such as "irrational exuberance" or "froth" to describe the overheated market. Professionals start selling their overpriced stocks to confident mechanics and pizza-shop owners. To cool down the economy, the Federal Reserve raises interest rates so that fewer people can get loans to buy homes, cars etcetera. With this decline in business – or in anticipation of it – stocks drop slightly. Professionals buy bonds or put their money in cash.

Retail investors don't worry about the decline in stocks, because they know that the economy is doing spectacularly well – the media says so. Stocks drop more. Retail investors remain confident. Stocks drop more. Although they begin to worry, they remind themselves that they are "long-term investors" and will simply wait for prices to rise again. Mutual fund managers and bankers tell people to "hang on" and not sell, since at this low stage it is better to wait for the rebound. Analysts warn of a difficult market. Consumers spend less. Stocks drop further still. Finally, unable to sleep at night, retail investors begin unloading their mutual funds and stocks.

Waves of selling bring reduced prices and still more selling. Panic sets in. Financial news anchors start to babble hysterically and argue with their guests. News agencies announce that we are now in a recession, that life is terrible, and that the horrors may never end. Retail stock writers pen articles warning people that they may lose "everything."

After days or weeks of frightening stories, financial news anchors finally run out of adrenaline and become gloomy and exhausted. The evening news tells the story of the lady next door who saves money by some new and ingenious method.

Shortly thereafter, Wall Street professionals realize that the stock market has hit a low plateau – all the retail investors have finished selling! Professionals buy. As they are buying, they make TV appearances warning retail investors not to buy, since it is still very risky (this allows professionals time to buy stocks before the return of retail money raises prices).

And so the cycle continues…whether with stocks, oil, gold, real estate, tulip bulbs, or frozen concentrated orange juice. Although everyone knows that to make money in the market you have to "buy low and sell high," most investors do exactly the opposite. Retail investors are so afraid of losing money that they consistently lose money.

To be successful in the market, you must conquer your fears surrounding money. You must buy low and sell high, which, in practice, is "buy pessimism and sell euphoria." You have to buy at a time when everyone else is afraid to do so – but not too soon.

"Buy when everyone else is selling and hold until everyone else is buying…it is the very essence of successful investment."

J. Paul Getty

Why Mutual Funds Under-Perform

You may have heard that, on average, professionally managed mutual funds provide lower average returns than the overall market: this is the "dirty secret of mutual funds," and it is true. Partly this lack of performance is due to management expenses that cut into profits. Partly it is because some strategies (and some fund managers) are better than others. But primarily, managed mutual funds consistently under-perform the broader market because of the demands of their clients.

A retail investor typically wants to see the value of their portfolio increase every quarter, regardless of market conditions, and regardless of their time horizon. That is, they do not want to see the value of their portfolio fluctuate (downward) in any three-month period, even if they plan to keep the money invested for another 20 years. Psychologists call this phenomenon "myopic loss aversion," a reference to myopia, the technical term for shortsightedness. Whatever the name, this strange psychological quirk destroys a mutual fund manager's probability of success, and the client's probability of success along with it.

Because of short-term focus, mutual fund managers are forced to do inane things. For example, when markets decline and great buying opportunities abound, scared clients take their money out of mutual funds. This forces mutual fund managers to liquidate stocks instead of buying more, or to hold large amounts in cash to pay out fleeing clients.

Some managers, dreading their client's wrath, sell under-performing stocks just before the end of each quarter and buy stocks that have been performing well. This way, clients can see a nice list of successful companies when they get their quarterly statements. Managers sell their under-performers no matter how solid they may be as long-term prospects. After the statements have gone out, these same managers will sell all the nice-looking stocks they just bought and re-purchase the ones they just sold. Such "window dressing" creates high transaction costs and turnover rates.

And finally, the *coupe de grace*: "closet indexing." Battered by constantly being asked, "Why am I losing money?" and "Why didn't you beat the index last quarter?" managers simply give up and buy the stocks in an index. That way, although they will never beat the index (which is what they are being paid to do), they will never lag behind it too much either.

Successful mutual fund managers know that although managing stocks is important, managing clients is also important; and, the best way to manage clients is to give them what they want, regardless of how much it hurts them.

The Consequences of Fear

Actual Comments from Investors, March 2009*

"This depression is different. We've fallen off a cliff, and we don't know what the outcome will be. I think we will eventually recover but we'll never be a great country again."

"We will rent a safe deposit box and put all our cash into that safe deposit box. This credit issue is far from over, and it's much too dangerous to leave the funds invested."

"Sure, money market funds and CD's yield very little, but at least the principal amount is always there."

"If I'd stuck the money under my mattress I would have 40% more than the actual value of my account today."

"[President] Barack Obama is a great liar. Most people who voted for him don't realize they were lied to. They think the [economic] stimulus package will actually help the economy."

"Obama is a liar. There is great evil in this man. Only time will tell whether or not he is the anti-Christ."

"Our children will never know what freedom is. In a few years the USA will not exist."

"Here is my advice .. Get out of the stock market now! Save whatever you have left."

"I can't wait for the market to recover. I'm 70 years old. By the time the market recovers, I'll be dead."

"All I was doing was watching [news station] all day, hoping for signs that the market would go up. I was shouting at my kids and fighting with my wife. The stress was unbearable. Finally, I couldn't take it anymore. I sold out and lost 80% of my money."

"The worst is yet to come. There will be food shortages, civil unrest, riots in the streets. This is the end of capitalism."

"It's possible that stocks will never recover."

Author's note: In the 12 months following these comments, the U.S. stock market went up 66.7%

*edited for grammar, spelling, and readability

What is Risk?

According to prevailing economic theory, "risk" is the volatility of a stock or stock portfolio; that is, risk is defined as how much the price moves up and down. The higher the volatility is, the greater the risk.

Most investors do not view risk in the same way. To most people, "risk" is not the likelihood that a stock will be volatile (since they have no concerns when a stock goes up). Risk is purely the probability of seeing their investment values decline. Specifically, most people are uncomfortable seeing the values of their investments drop below their previous highs.

Exceptional investors view risk as neither volatility nor the probability of decline. Lacking fear, they use a more sensible definition: risk is the probability of a permanent loss of capital.

Portfolio Theory & Asset Allocation

Modern Portfolio Theory is the idea that the overall portfolio mix – and not the merit of each investment – is the most important consideration. According to modern portfolio theory, if an investment portfolio is comprised of different classes of assets (stocks of different sectors, bonds etc) then the overall riskiness of the portfolio is reduced ("Risk," in this case, is defined as "volatility.")

For a risk-averse investor, a comfortable portfolio might be 20% stocks, 40% bonds and 40% cash. For an investor who is moderately risk-averse, a portfolio of 40% stocks, 40% bonds and 20% cash may be better. Over several years, probability is high that the risk-averse investor will make less than the moderately risk-averse investor, who will make less than the risk-tolerant investor.

It is important to recognize that although asset allocation is a way to manage people's money, it is also a way to manage people. It is a way to control the fear of monetary loss for people who are unable to control this fear themselves, and for this reason it is valuable.

Investors who have overcome their fear of "losing money" (i.e. seeing their principle temporarily decline) have more limited use for portfolio theory. Sometimes this means that they are 100% invested in stocks (though of course never at the peak of a market cycle). At other times it means they will have most of their money in cash, when no good investments are available. Investments are made based on the merit of each investment at a given point in time.

"Our capital is under-utilized right now. It's a painful position to be in, but not as painful as doing something stupid."

Warren Buffett

The Noodle Man of Edo

In the old city of Edo, now known as Tokyo, three businessmen started a noodle shop on a busy street. Their noodles were tasty, and soon the business was thriving.

One day, the first partner arrived looking sorrowful. "What's wrong?" the other two partners asked. "I just heard that the Shogun is raising taxes on silk," the first partner said. "Surely, people will have less money to spend, and our business will suffer. I would like to sell my share." The other two partners agreed to buy out his share for a small sum (surely less than the business was worth in good times), and all were happy.

The remaining two partners continued to work hard every day. Their business slowed for a few months, just as the first partner had predicted, but soon returned. In fact, the business became so successful that they each saved much gold.

One day, the second partner arrived at the noodle shop looking worried. "What is wrong?" the third partner asked. "I heard that there is a rebellion in the South," the second partner said. "Surely, the samurai will be sent to fight, and our business will suffer. I would like to sell my share." The third partner offered to buy out the second partner for a small sum (surely less than the business was worth in good times), and both were happy.

The samurai were indeed sent to quell the rebellion; however, they achieved a swift victory and returned to Edo. The noodle shop became even busier than before. The business was so successful that the owner saved much gold.

One day, the owner read that grain fields throughout Japan had been ruined by typhoons. Foolishly, he did not heed the news, nor did he buy extra grain in anticipation of higher prices to come. That year, his noodle shop and many others like it were forced to raise prices. Business suffered badly.

Despite his mistakes, the owner had saved so much gold during the previous period of prosperity that his business survived, and he was able to buy three other noodle shops for a small sum (surely less than the businesses were worth in good times). All were happy.

In time, he became one of the wealthiest men in Edo.

Unwise investment decisions, based upon emotion, pursue unskilled investors relentlessly.

The Shopkeeper and the Fortune-Teller

A shopkeeper went to see a fortune-teller, who told the shopkeeper that her business in the coming year would not be successful. She was stunned and saddened, since her business had theretofore been growing rapidly.

The next day, the businesswoman stayed in bed for most of the morning. "There is no point waking early," she said to her children, "since my business will not be profitable this year."

When she finally went to her shop, she found her employees playing games instead of working. Ordinarily she would have scolded them for doing so, but this day she did not. "There is no reason to scold them," she thought, "since even if they work harder my business will not make money."

At the end of the year, the shopkeeper tallied her earnings and expenditures. "My business was unprofitable!" she said aloud. "That fortune teller is the greatest!"

Opportunity Cost

"Opportunity cost" is a relatively straightforward concept: it states that for every decision that you make, you should consider the consequences of not making an alternative decision. Opportunity cost is the cost of not taking advantage of opportunities, and of not putting your potential financial resources to their best uses.

Although opportunity cost is usually expressed in terms of money, it is in fact far more useful. It can be used to help make better decisions about anything of value; which means, to make decisions about life.

Consider the following examples:

You can either work for four years, or get a university degree. If you choose working, you will gain four years of pay and experience, incur no debt, but forego the increased earning potential, personal contacts and mental development you would have gained in university.

You put a down payment on a rental suite. Afterward, you find a nicer and less expensive rental suite, and decide to take it. The down payment was the cost of the opportunity to have extra time to look for a better suite, while holding it in case you didn't.

You pay for a meal at a restaurant. You save time, perhaps enjoy a better meal than you could have prepared yourself, but forego money that could have been saved or used for something else.

You put your money in an investment that gives you 2% interest (such as a term bank account), even though it could have been invested in something that gives you 4% interest with little or no additional risk. You are earning 2% interest on your money. But, you have also lost the opportunity to earn an extra 2% on your money.

You own a vacation property in Hawaii, and you aren't going to use it this year. You have neither gained nor lost money by not using it, since you already own it. But, from an opportunity cost point of view, you have lost money.

An experienced engineer decides to change careers and start his own small business, as sole proprietor. As an engineer, the man earned x dollars per year. As owner, his business expects to earn half that amount per year. Because the man could have earned double his current income as an engineer, he suffers an opportunity cost for his career change. This monetary opportunity cost may (or may not) be offset by the greater freedom and sense of satisfaction gained as a sole proprietor.

When most people make decisions about their home, their workplace, or their investments, they only think about what they are spending or earning, without considering the alternatives in a comprehensive manner.

The purpose of opportunity cost is not to dwell on the stock you didn't buy, or the job you didn't take. It should, however, be used to actively think about your life and its decisions. Are your investments doing as well as they could be? Are you paying for a lifestyle that you really don't need or possibly can't afford? Are you satisfied with your income, or is there anything you can do to improve it? Not only with investments, but also with every other important decision, you should use opportunity cost to weigh your decisions honestly and truthfully.

The Painting

One fine day in London, a pauper, a businessman, and an aristocrat each decided to buy a painting to decorate his home.

The pauper went to a dry goods store and bought canvas, framing, a brush, and some paint. He then went to the park, to create the painting by his own hand.

The businessman went to a boutique art dealer and chose a painting by a known local artist, which was skillfully painted, if not entirely original. The businessman paid a full days' income.

The aristocrat went to a famous auction house, where the works of several old masters were presented. He spent the whole day bidding, until one of his bids was successful. The amount he paid was substantial.

At the end of the day, the three compared their purchases.

Upon seeing the businessman's painting the pauper asked, "Why would you spend so much, when you could have painted it yourself?"

Upon seeing the aristocrat's painting the businessman asked, "Why would you spend so much, when you could have bought a beautiful work like mine for a fraction of the price?"

The aristocrat explained his decision. "You spent a little," he said to the pauper, "which was wise." "You spent much," he said to the businessman, "which was unwise." "But I," the aristocrat continued, "did not spend anything at all."

Investment Styles

For many investors, undoubtedly the most confusing thing about investing is that there are so many different styles of investing, and so many conflicting strategies. There is momentum investing, technical analysis, day trading, buy-and-hold, asset allocation, value investing, index investing and many others. Which one is the best? Or, is there such a thing as "best?"

The easiest way to explain methods of investment is to use the comparison of a person wanting to become fit or lose weight. There are hundreds, perhaps thousands, of different ways to lose weight, and each person has their own opinion on which is best.

The most proven and longest-lasting method for losing weight is well known: eat healthier than you are eating now, and be more active than you are now. Despite this simplicity, however, almost no one does it. It's easy to sit around the home instead of being active. It's addictive and comforting to eat foods high in fat and sugar. Thus, despite knowing which method is the most effective, cognitive dissonance comes into play, and most people do everything in their power to believe in something other than what is necessary.

Instead of eating healthier and becoming more active, people take pills or drink special teas; they buy cheap exercise toys; they even buy motorized machines that move their limbs for them. They engage in special diets such as eating nothing but grapefruits, eliminating all cereals and grains from their diet, or drinking protein milkshakes instead of meals. These latter methods tend to gain popularity quickly since they garner quick results, even though the results are unsustainable.

In the 1970s, a popular diet was to eat high amounts of protein and almost no carbohydrates. Many athletes, in particular, joined the high protein diet fad. At first, the results were promising. After several months, however, the athletes found that their bodies began to smell. Starving from lack of carbohydrates, their bodies began converting protein into usable energy, the by-product of which was ammonia. Despite all this, thirty years later the "high-protein low-carbohydrate" diet came back into fashion.

So it is with investing (or, more accurately, investing and speculating). There are many methods for investing, and there are advocates for each method. Some methods do not work at all, yet they persist; others offer quick but unsustainable results; still others give steady results that last. These latter investment styles – which offer steady results that last – tend to be avoided, since they require a level of self-control, effort and patience that most people simply do not possess.

In the following pages, we break down the most common investment styles.

Momentum Investing

Momentum investing is the art of investing in companies that are growing rapidly, and whose stock prices are also growing rapidly. For example, you may buy a company where, in every quarter for the past two years, earnings have grown by 20% or higher (any number in excess of the average corporate growth rate). Such stocks tend to sell well above their net asset and earnings values, due to expectations of rapid growth. Put another way, momentum investing *requires* that one buy overpriced stocks, in the belief that earnings will catch up. An excellent example of this is the large number of Internet stocks traded from 1997-2000. The sales growth rate for many of these companies was tremendous, and their stocks reflected this growth with high prices in relation to book value, and price/earning ratios up to infinity.

In some instances, momentum investing works, and works well. Those who bought Internet stocks in 1997 and sold them in 2000 made huge fortunes. The problem with momentum investing is that no one knows when the good times will end, and therefore no one knows when to get out. It is, as Warren Buffett explains, like a "Cinderella Party," where everything will eventually turn to pumpkins. Everyone knows it, yet no one wants to be the first to leave.

A single quarter of lower than expected earnings can crush a momentum stock.

Technical Analysis

Technical analysis, or charting, is the use of charts and past price movements to determine the future direction of stocks. One common example of technical analysis is the use of a "moving average," which is the average price over a certain time period (for example, the average price over the last 52 weeks). If a stock crosses under its moving average, it is expected to continue falling. If a stock crosses over its moving average, it is expected to continue rising. An example is shown in the chart below.

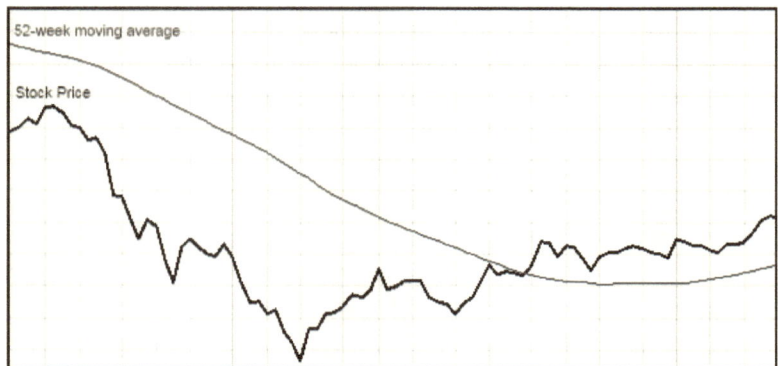

On a very basic level, technical analysis works. For example, if a stock has been dropping daily for two weeks straight, it will likely continue dropping because it is clearly being sold off. If a stock crosses above its 52-week moving average, chances are that some aspect of the company or the market has changed, and the price rise should continue. Many investors look at charts, at this basic level, to determine at what point they should buy or sell. The devil with technical analysis is, however, in the details.

Advocates of technical analysis believe that stock charts can quickly and accurately predict price moves, by how much and by when. They believe that a chart – and the chart alone – is all that is necessary to buy or sell a stock. That is, without researching what may have caused the stock's price to change, or even knowing what the company does, they will buy or sell a stock since "the chart tells all." In this sense, technical analysis is akin to fortune telling.

Chartists memorize patterns and give them names like, "the cup and saucer," "the evening star," and "the head and shoulders formation." Since the human mind is known to search for patterns (even where none exist), the search for such technical patterns is always successful.

Despite negligible proof that detailed technical analysis works, brokerages commonly encourage its use. Charting inevitably leads to a large volume of buying and selling (charts are always changing), which is great for generating commissions. Brokerages frequently offer free technical analysis courses. Technical trading may not be the best way for an investor to make money, but it is certainly one of the best ways for Wall Street to make money.

Professional technical traders (employed by brokerage houses) enjoy the sense of fraternity that comes with knowing about, and believing in, this complicated trading style. Since it is an active method, it also keeps traders busy and gives them something to do. Successful trading requires hordes of time and attention.

Day Trading

Day trading is the art of buying and selling stocks within the day. Stocks are not held overnight, but are instead traded like cards in Poker: sometimes being held for hours, sometimes for no more than a few seconds. Day traders may trade based on trading volume, charts (using technical analysis), news, or on essentially anything that they feel will affect the short-term movement of a stock.

Day trading promises large gains in a short period of time. Of course, the alternative is also true – day trading can result in large losses in a short period of time. Since trading is fast and frequent, brokerages love day traders and the commissions they generate. Anecdotally, it is understood that most active day traders lose their entire invested capital within the first year.

Buy-and-Hold

"Buy-and-hold" is not really an investment style, as much as a practical admonition to retail investors. Since retail investors tend to sell their stocks at the worst possible time (after prices have already dropped), buy-and-hold is taught as a technique to overcome it. Specifically, retail investors are told to buy a stock or mutual fund, and "hang on" no matter what happens. Although this is far from being a great investment method, it is better than the alternative – selling at the point of panic.

For value investors, buy-and-hold has a different meaning. Buy-and-hold means to buy the stock of a great company, and then hold on to it for as long as the reasons for buying it remain true. As the company grows and develops, the stock price usually grows and develops along with it. However, if a stock becomes grossly overpriced (for example, having a P/E ratio of 30 or higher), if the company's strategy or management changes for the worse, or if there are accounting irregularities, the investor will sell the stock. "Hold" only means hold for as long as a great company remains a great company.

Brokerages typically mock and discourage the buy-and-hold method, since it results in very low trading revenues. Mutual fund companies typically encourage the buy-and-hold method, since fund managers are paid based on balances and not trading.

Asset Allocation

Asset allocation is a technique whereby stocks are bought and sold based on the business cycle. For example, at low points in the business cycle, cyclical companies such as auto and appliance manufacturers are purchased. At the mid point in the cycle, consumer and growth companies such as brokerages and restaurants are purchased. Finally, at the high point in the cycle, "defensive stocks" like utility companies are purchased, because they pay high dividends and tend to keep their value in a falling market. In the asset allocation strategy, the company is not as important as the segment that the company falls under – for example, defensive, cyclical, or growth.

Asset allocation sounds very practical and straightforward. In practice, investors have difficulty judging which stage of the cycle the market is at, confuse short cycles with long ones, and frequently buy and sell the wrong types of companies at the wrong times. Due to trading costs and taxes, asset allocation investors regularly under-perform the general market.

Value Investing

Value investing has consistently provided investors with superior returns with minimal risk over long periods of time.

Value investing is the technique of selecting stocks in the same way that one would buy entire enterprises. For example, the stock (company) cannot be overpriced, as measured either by the P/E ratio, or the price to book value. It should be a company with proven, stable earnings that has survived previous recessions. It should have little or no long-term debt. The products or services provided should be practical and simple, with little chance that a new and innovative competitor could take its business away. In value investing, any quality that makes a company attractive makes its stock attractive.

Most value investors employ the buy-and-hold technique, meaning that they buy businesses with great qualities, and then hold them until they either become overvalued, lose their competitive edge, or until an even better investment opportunity presents itself. Value investors believe that market crashes are a gift, since they result in vast quantities of newly undervalued stocks.

A Sample Value Investing Checklist

1. The company has been in business for more than 10 years.
2. The company has had 4 quarters or less of negative earnings in the last 10 years.
3. P/E ratio is less than 15.
4. Long-term Debt/Equity ratio is less than 0.20
5. Quick Ratio is greater than 1.0
6. Return On Equity is greater than 15.
7. No major new share issuances in the past 2 years.

There are several negative points to value investing, all primarily psychological. Firstly, value investing requires an unusual level of patience. An undervalued stock can stay undervalued for years, even as the company itself expands and grows. Value investing is also counterintuitive, which causes some people an unbearable amount of stress. Supreme confidence is required to buy stocks of companies to which analysts have given "sell" ratings, and which friends and neighbors ignore or despise. And of course, value investing demands that investors read the "boring" financial statements, annual reports, and press releases. These days, some unscrupulous companies, knowing what value investors are looking for, use creative accounting to build their financial statements to suit. Proper diligence and effort is required.

New value investors should be mindful of the "value trap." That is, be aware that cyclical companies may show excellent numbers at the peak of a market cycle, making them look like bargains when in fact they are not.

For those with the time, inclination, and psychological strength to do it, value investing pays off strikingly well.

Index Investing

Index investing was intentionally saved for last. Although index investing is not the *best* investment strategy, for many people it is the best *practical* investment strategy.

Generally, only large, strong companies who are leaders in their fields are admitted to an index. The S&P 500, for example, is comprised of 500 of the largest companies on North American markets. Buying stocks from an index is therefore, in itself, a method of choosing good stocks.

The primary issue with index investing is that, occasionally, an entire index can become overpriced. In 2000, for example, technology stocks became obscenely overpriced and, since the NASDAQ exchange held the largest technology companies, the NASDAQ index itself became obscenely overpriced. When it finally fell, it lost 65% of its value in less than a year.

Despite its limitations, however, index investing is a smart and practical way to invest in stocks, and minimizes the potential for failure. An example of a wise index-investing program follows:

Step 1. Buy a "bond index mutual fund," or Exchange-Traded Fund that follows a large and diversified index such as the DEX Universe Bond Index. The Fund or ETF you choose should have low fees (a Management Expense Ratio of less than 1%). Invest the percentage of your total investment capital equivalent to your age. For example, if you are 40, invest 40% of your total capital in a bond index fund. The interest earned from the bond index fund should be reinvested in the next fund – the stock index fund.

Step 2. Using the remainder of your capital, buy a "stock index mutual fund" or Exchange-Traded Fund that follows a large and diversified stock index, such as the S&P 500 or the Russell 2000. Again, the Management Expense Ratio should be under 1%.

Step 3. Buy and hold. If the stock market drops, the interest income from the Bond fund will allow you to buy stocks at reduced prices, making a drop more of a blessing than a curse. If you wish to add to your existing holdings, simply repeat Steps 1 and 2. After large market crashes, consider buying more.

For those unwilling (or unable) to put in the time and effort necessary for value investing, index investing is a simple way to obtain excellent returns with minimal time and effort.

Conclusion

It should be apparent that this author believes value Investing and index investing are the most effective methods of investment (some would argue, all else is speculation). However, this does not necessarily mean that you should adopt one of these styles to the exclusion of all others.

If you drive fast, smoke cigarettes, and like to gamble, chances are that you will never be satisfied purely as a buy-and-hold investor, no matter how lucrative it is. Likewise, if you are a calm intellectual, rarely or never gamble, and are faithful to your spouse, you will likely not be successful as a trader.

The primary investment style you choose (using the bulk of your money) should be based on logic. The secondary investment style you choose can be based on your personality. Know your personality, and then choose your investment styles accordingly.

How Much to Invest?

In any single stock, never invest an amount more than you are completely comfortable losing. If you invest a thousand dollars in a single stock, ensure you would be comfortable losing this amount. If you invest a million dollars in a single stock, ensure you would be comfortable losing this amount. History has shown that even the most benign investment can be overcome by disaster, and expecting this – or at least being prepared for it – means that you are already ahead.

In any combination of stocks, never invest an amount more than you would feel comfortable with if it were to drop by 50-60%, since history shows that this is possible. Put another way, you should be in a position to see your stocks drop by 50% and still be financially (and mentally) secure. As a rule, investors who have never experienced a severe market crash completely underestimate the trauma they will feel when it happens.

If you invest more than you are prepared to lose, you will experience anxiety during the fluctuations that always accompany investments, and will therefore make unwise decisions. Avoiding bad decisions is of equal or greater value than making good ones.

One of the great secrets of investing is that in order to gain, one must be prepared to lose.

"I consider it the duty of every serious investor to suffer grievous losses with great equanimity."

John Maynard Keynes

The Person Paradigm

If a person owned a long-established shipping company, with a fleet of ships and a solid balance sheet, and asked you for a loan, would you give it to him? On the other hand, if someone said that they drilled a hole in a local mountain and found evidence of diamonds, would you give that person the same amount of money? For some reason, people throw money at risky companies that they would never give to an individual under the same circumstances.

As far back as 1928, Napoleon Hill recognized that people were more likely to give charitable donations to a third party than to give money to the person requiring the charity directly. When investing, people have a similar reaction – they are far less scrutinizing when buying a company's stock than they would be if investing in a company directly. In fact, it is safe to say that people often take longer to choose a new pair of shoes than they do to invest thousands of dollars in company stock.

In order to combat the aforementioned weakness of human character, it is useful to think of the company you are investing in as if it were an individual asking you for a personal investment. Therefore, before making any stock purchase, ask yourself, "If someone came to me as owner of a company with the same story, would I give them the same amount of money?" Think of your money as being invested with an individual, and you are less likely to make foolish mistakes.

"Success is a lousy teacher. It seduces smart people into thinking they can't lose."

Bill Gates

The Probability Method

Imagine a fair coin toss, where if you guess the result (heads or tails) correctly, you get $1000. If you guess incorrectly, you lose $900. Would you do it?

Most people say "no," to the coin toss bet. Yet, provided that you can afford to lose $900 several times and remain in good financial condition, this is precisely the type of risk that you – and every smart investor – should look for.

In this coin toss example, there is a 50% chance of getting $1000 on every toss, or (.50 x $1000) = $500. There is also a 50% chance of losing $900 on every toss (.50 x $900) = -$450. In other words, on multiple coin tosses, you are likely to make an average of $50 for each coin toss. You could choose heads or tails, and then toss coins all day long and quickly become a millionaire.

Many people invest in "long shots" such as gold mines or other risky investments without analyzing the probabilities of success. But, taking the time to do so will add clarity to your investment decisions, and help you steer clear of avoidable mistakes influenced by emotions.

As an example, consider investing in a gold mine, of which only one successful drill hole (core sample) has been made. Say, based on your experience and research that the probability of a promising drill hole becoming a functioning mine is only 1 in 100, or 1%. The stock is currently trading at $0.50, and based on rudimentary analysis you believe that if the mine were to become operational, the existing stock (considering the effects of dilution) would rise to $5.00 per share. If the mine were unsuccessful, however, the stock would fall to $.10 before being bought out by another company.

You are considering a purchase of $10,000. Should you invest?

$10,000 buys 20,000 shares at $0.50 each. There is a 1% chance (by your estimation) that the stock price will rise to $5.00, giving you a profit of $90,000 (20,000 shares x gain of $4.50 per share). There is a 99% chance that the stock price will drop to $0.10, giving you a loss of $8000 (20,000 shares x loss of $0.40 per share). The final calculation is therefore (.01 x $90,000) – (0.99 x $8000) or ($900 - $7920) = -$7020. If you were to make this "investment" repeatedly, you stand to lose an average of $7020 every time. Obviously, this is an investment you should pass up.

Before making any investment, ask yourself questions such as these:

- What is the probability that the company (not stock) will be successful?
- What could derail this company's success?
- If the company were to become more successful, how much more successful could it be?
- Is the company based around a single product or service, or around multiple products or services?
- Do consumers feel an emotional attachment to the company or its brands?
- Is the company based around a charismatic leader? What would happen to the company if disaster struck its leader?
- How much debt does the company have?
- Does the company have enough cash for near-term operating expenses?
- How long has the company been in business?
- How big of a threat are the company's current competitors?
- Could a new competitor take away their business?
- Has their business model changed significantly in recent years?
- How might my ideas about this company be wrong?

Estimating an investment's probability of success will always be, at best, an educated guess. Nonetheless, the process itself will force you to scrutinize your investment decisions carefully, weeding out investments that are not worth your time or money. Extraordinarily diligence results in extraordinary gains.

In investing, as in sports, winning is not about making the most spectacular plays, but rather about making the fewest errors.

Case Study: Citigroup

In 2007, the financial world was struck by a crisis unseen since the Great Crash 78 years earlier. US real estate prices had risen first by a combination of demand and financial innovation, then by shortage, then by greed. When the mortgage bubble burst, the result was mass unemployment and the "credit crisis." One of the companies caught in the middle of this crisis was Citigroup® Inc.

Citigroup held a large number of overpriced assets related to housing. When the price of these assets fell, Citigroup found itself grossly undercapitalized (banks are required to keep a certain ratio of capital to loans). Citigroup needed help, desperately.

The government stepped in, buying up a large portion of the company and in effect, partially (but not completely) nationalizing it. The President of the United States, as well as the Treasury Secretary, publicly stated that they would not let America's largest banks fail, and that they would not be fully nationalized. Despite this, financial commentators could be seen everywhere on television and in print, telling investors that banks would go bankrupt, and to stay away.

Citigroup stock fell from a high of $55 in 2007 to a low of $1 in 2009. Despite successful recapitalization and repeated government assurances, Citigroup languished in the $3-5 range for months. So, how was one to tell if Citigroup stock was a good buy? Was it worth the risk?

First, we must think about the risk of failure at that time. Although Citigroup was unprofitable it was also well-capitalized, meaning that it could likely withstand several quarters of negative earnings without incident. Its international network of branches and associated client base was largely intact. Just as importantly, the government had publicly stated that Citigroup would not be allowed to fail. Armed with these facts, we can roughly estimate the probability of failure to be about 10%; or alternatively, give a 90% chance that Citigroup will not go bankrupt within one market cycle.

Following this section are the earnings of Citigroup for 2005-2009. During peak earnings in 2005, Citigroup earned $4.84 per share. Assuming that this was an anomaly caused by the housing boom, and that these earnings would not be seen again for some time, a conservative estimate would be that only 70% of the former earnings, or $3.39 per share, would be likely in the next market cycle.

Since Citigroup also had bad publicity during the crisis, a very conservative estimate was that 30% of the clients and staff would leave and not come back in the near future, again hurting earnings (in fact, the income sheet suggests that this was unlikely, but overly conservative estimates are always better). Therefore, use only 70% of the previous figure ($3.39), or now $2.37 per share.

Then there are the shares themselves. In 2005, Citigroup had 5.067 billion shares, but during the credit crisis they issued a tremendous number of new shares (to raise funds to save themselves), and so by the end of 2009, 11.568 billion shares were outstanding – 2.29 times more. Therefore, our new estimate of $2.37 per share becomes only $1.04 per share, since the earnings are now spread between more shares.

When people are relatively optimistic but not exuberant, the P/E ratio of the market is about 15. Therefore, with our earnings of $1.04 per share, we can estimate that by the end of the next market cycle (which may take several years), Citigroup will be priced at about $15.60 per share ($1.04 x 15).

You are considering an investment of $5000 in Citibank stock at $4 per share, which would buy 1250 shares (excluding commissions).

The final conclusion is thus:

10% probability of losing everything to bankruptcy:
$5000 x probability of .10 = -$500

90% probability of the stock going to $15.60:
Delta of $11.60 per share (a rise from $4 to $15.60) x 1250 shares x probability of .90 = $13,050

-$500 + $13,050 = $12,550

According to these very conservative estimates, every time you make a $5000 investment in a company like Citibank in 2009, you have the probability of more than doubling your money over one market cycle. This investment is as good as it gets.

Annual Income Statement (Currency: US$Mil) Citigroup Inc.

Income Statement	31-Dec-09	31-Dec-08	31-Dec-07	31-Dec-06	31-Dec-05
Total Revenue	**108006**	105756	159229	146558	**120318**
Cost of Goods Sold	10146	20271	0	0	0
Gross Profit	97860	85485	159229	146558	120318
R & D Expense	0	0	0	0	0
Selling & Admin. Expenses	88197	104082	77534	59976	54209
EBITDA	9776	-20363	79232	86582	66109
Depreciation & Amortization	0	0	0	0	0
Interest Expense	17575	32692	77531	56943	36676
Income before Tax	-7799	-53055	1701	29639	29433
Income Tax	-6733	-20612	-2201	8101	9078
Minority Interest	N/A	N/A	N/A	N/A	N/A
Investment Gains/Losses	0	0	0	0	0
Other After Tax Adjusts	0	0	0	0	0
Profit/Loss	-1606	-27684	3617	21538	24589
Earnings Per Share($)	-0.8	-3.88	0.72	4.31	**4.84**
Diluted Earnings per Share	-0.8	-3.88	0.72	4.31	4.75
Avg Shares Outstanding	**11,568,000,000**	4,823,454,000	5,027,778,000	4,997,680,000	**5,067,600,000**

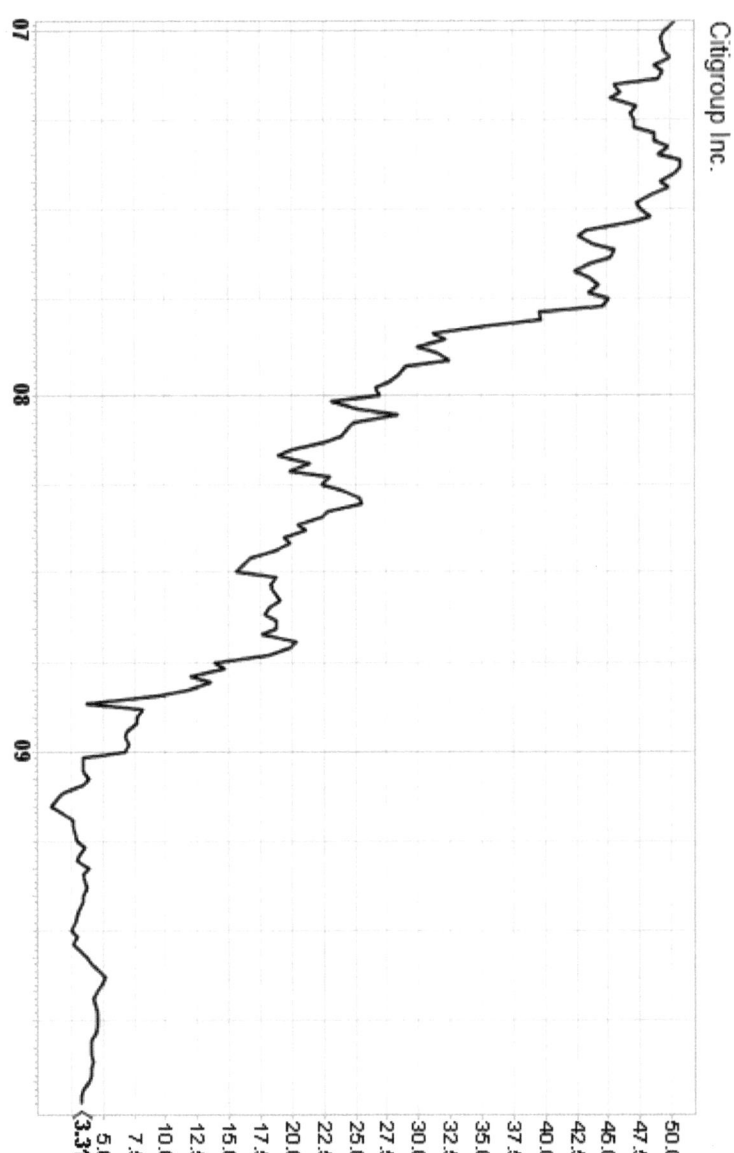

Citigroup Inc.

Compound Growth

Result of investing $50,000 and keeping it for 20 years:

> At 1% (Bank account rate)
> $61,009.50
> At 3% (GIC / T-Bill rate)
> $90,305.56
> At 6% (Corporate Bond Rate)
> $160,356.72
> At 10% (Long-term stock market rate)
> $336,375.00
> At 15% (Active Value investing rate)
> $818,326.83

Result of investing $100/month for 20 years (Total investment of $24,000):

> At 1% (Bank account rate)
> $26,543.69
> At 3% (GIC / T-Bill rate)
> $32,685.44
> At 6% (Corporate Bond Rate)
> $45,343.92
> At 10% (Long-term stock market rate)
> $71,825.92
> At 15% (Active Value investing rate)
> $131,170.69

"…if any reader of these chapters is convinced – really convinced – he cannot master the market, a great deal has been accomplished, because the great majority will fail in the market, and it's worth dollars and cents for them to know it."

Gerald Loeb

Part V – Words of Warning

The Scholar Who Knew Nothing

In a district near Nanjing lived a poor young man who wished to become greater. He spent months in the shelter of an ancient ruin, studying religion, art, history, and philosophy, hoping to pass the examinations to become a government official. One day, he ignored nature's cold elements too much and was struck with weakness, his lips quivering and his skin blue.

When he awoke, he found himself in the hut of a stranger, next to a fire. A young woman was preparing for him a broth of rice and ginger. "I was nearly frozen," he said. "You have saved my life, and I am grateful." The young woman's father soon returned home, and welcomed the young man into his house.

In time the young man fell in love with the young woman, and they were married. With his wife's love and encouragement, the young man began studying again, and within the year passed the difficult imperial examinations. He was to pack his things, and move to the capital with his wife and her father. How fortunate he was!

They traveled toward the capital by boat. But on the journey, the ambitious young man's mind began to wander. "I am now an important official," he thought. "How can I be seen with a woman of no birthright, and her humble father? I will not be taken seriously, and my progress will be hindered if I keep this record of my origins." He decided that something must be done.

While his wife was peering over the edge of the boat into the water, the young man pushed her in. "Aiiyah!" The young man howled to the father. "My wife has fallen in, please help me save her!" As her father jumped up to help, the young man pushed him into the cold water also.

The young man continued to the capital, and was well received. He worked diligently every day. Within a few months, a matchmaker told him that the Minister of Justice wished to take him as a son-in-law, to which the young man readily agreed. "Now," he thought, "I am to be married to someone of proper standing."

On the evening of the ceremony, the young man approached his bride, lifting the silk veil to reveal her face. "Ghost!!" he cried out. "Ghost!" For within the veil was the face of his departed wife.

"Why is it that you cry 'Ghost?'" the minister asked. But, before the young man could answer, his wife's father walked into the hall as well. The young man realized that these were not ghosts, but that his wife and father had survived, and that the Minister knew what he had done. He dropped to his knees before the Minister. "Forgive me," the young man begged.

"You studied hard to become an official," the Minister said. "You have studied justice and honorable conduct, modesty and goodwill. You have studied much, learned much, but understood nothing."

The young man was punished severely for his crime, and only upon the mercy of his wife and her father was his life spared.

Warren and the Leopard

Once upon a time, a young man named Warren sat in the forest, pondering his future. Out of the trees a leopard stealthily crept up to him, but then sat down, swishing its tail contentedly, clearly meaning no harm.

Warren noted the leopard's long, slim profile, its elegant form, and its shiny coat. "What a magnificent pet this would make!" he exclaimed. Warren had a piece of rope, and wrapped it around the leopard's neck to use as a leash. "Now we can walk back to the village," he said to the leopard. The leopard happily followed along.

Soon, a small bird flew by. The leopard suddenly jumped at the bird, knocking Warren to the ground. "Please," Warren said to the leopard, "be more careful."

As they got closer to town, they passed a young woman taking a walk. The leopard looked angrily at the young woman, and sensed fear. Before Warren knew it, the leopard began pulling on the leash, scratching and snarling at the young woman. Only with all his might was Warren able to hold the leopard back. At that moment, he realized that it could not be.

He released the leopard from its leash, and bade it return to the forest, which it reluctantly did. "I was foolish," said Warren, "to walk a leopard on a leash, and believe I was in control."

Letter to J. Paul Getty, Age 83

"Dear Paul Getty:

You should not be living alone and as a bachelor –
not at your age and with your money. I am only 23,
blonde and healthy and strong. I could look after you.
I am willing to marry you for $100,000, cash payable
at the time of the wedding, plus $100,000 a year for
as long as you live. We can discuss the terms of your
will after you have sent me first-class airfare to come
to England. I enclose some candid photographs of
myself in the nude so you can see what you'll be
getting…"

The Lemonade Stand

Andrew, Barclay, and Christopher – three boys from the same neighborhood – decided to make some extra money during their summer holidays.   They would each start a lemonade stand, and see who would become the most successful!

Andrew started his business immediately.   He built a lemonade stand directly in front of his home, even though the street was usually quiet.   He made a sign saying, "Lemonade for Sale."   Barclay and Christopher decided to take a few days to do research about lemonade stands.   They learned which streets in the area had the most foot traffic; they found great recipes for lemonade; they questioned many adults and found out what they were willing to pay for a glass; and, they found a cheap supplier for their ingredients (their mother's kitchens).

By the end of the second week, Andrew had sold only a few glasses of lemonade, so he lost interest and quit.   Barclay launched his business, using the knowledge he had gained from the previous week.   He set up shop on a busy street corner a few blocks from his own house, and made a sign: "Lemon's Aid for Sale."   Many adults stopped to tell Barclay about his spelling error, and most of them bought lemonade. Christopher decided to take an extra week to develop a marketing strategy.

By the third week, Barclay's business was both profitable and successful, but his sales growth had stalled. Barclay hired a pessimist (his older brother) to review his business plan and offer advice.   Barclay's older brother was pleased to have the opportunity to tell his kid brother about all his mistakes and imperfections.   Barclay listened to his brother's words without emotion, and implemented many of his ideas.   Christopher decided to take an extra week to study bargaining techniques, strategic development, and long-term forecasting.

The fourth week, Barclay expanded his business by hiring a neighborhood boy to open a second location. Christopher took an extra week to study international sales and exporting requirements. He also hired a consulting firm to review his business plan.

By the end of the holidays, Barclay had earned enough money to buy an investment at his local bank: he would, in later years, retire as a multi-millionaire from these funds. Christopher used his money to buy candy.

The Broken Sparrow

A kind woman noticed a little sparrow trying unsuccessfully to fly. Upon examination, the woman found that it had broken its foot. She took the sparrow home, applied ointment to its foot, and fed it until it recovered. A few days later it flew away, in good health.

Not long after, it returned with a melon seed in its beak, which it dropped into the woman's lap. The woman planted the seed in the garden, and through the summer it grew into a healthy plant with a large watermelon.

On the day of her birthday, she took the tasty-looking watermelon from her garden in order to share it with her guests. But, when she opened it, she was astonished to find it filled with seeds of gold!

Her guests asked her to explain her remarkable story, which she gladly did. One woman was deeply envious, and decided to try the same luck for herself.

The envious woman caught a sparrow the very next day, and broke its foot. She then applied ointment to the foot, and spent her days caring for and feeding the sparrow until it had fully recovered. The same day the sparrow flew away.

Not long after, it returned with a melon seed in its beak, which it dropped into the woman's lap. The woman planted the seed in the garden, and it soon grew into a healthy plant with a large watermelon.

On an auspicious day, the woman invited all of her richest neighbors to celebrate at her home. She took the tasty-looking watermelon from her garden in order to share it with them. But, when she opened it, she was astonished to find it filled with snakes and centipedes! The creatures scurried from the melon, frightening her guests and biting them.

None of the guests returned to her home.

Epilogue

The Consequences of Monetary Success

Monetary success will bring you freedom. You can order the meal that you want, in the restaurant that you want. You can take a vacation to the place you want. You can send your children to a better school. You can care for others. Money is, for most people, a constant worry, and having it eliminates this worry.

Keep in mind, however, that true happiness depends on such things as good friends, family, and health. True happiness requires that you live ethically and morally, and can therefore sleep soundly without being beaten up by your conscience, and without the universe reminding you that you are ignoring it.

With reasonable ambition, sound judgment & lack of fear, monetary success will come. With morality, ethics, trustworthiness and empathy, you will keep it and be able to enjoy it.

"Ability will get you to the top, but it takes character to keep you there."

Abraham Lincoln

Bibliography

(1892, Dec. 3) Jay Gould's Career Ended. In *The New York Times*. New York, New York.

(1892, Dec. 3) Gould's Eventful Life. In *The New York Times*. New York, New York.

(1934, Nov. 1). 30,000 Attend Funeral of Chas. A. Floyd. In *Democrat-American*. Sallisaw, Oklahoma.

(2003, April 18). Cultural Obituaries: Sir Paul Getty. In *The Telegraph*. Retrieved from http://www.telegraph.co.uk/news/obituaries/culture-obituaries/1427781/Sir-Paul-Getty-obituary.html

Ammann, Daniel (2009). *The King of Oil*. New York: St. Martin's Press.

Barnett, R (1990). *The Idea of Higher Education*. Buckingham: Open University Press and SRHE.

Bergler, Edmund (1959). *Principles of Self-Damage.* New York: The Philosophical Library.

Bogle, John C. (2009). *Enough*. Hoboken, New Jersey: John Wiley and Sons.

Buddha, Shakyamuni (1993). *The Lotus Sutra* (Burton Watson, Trans.). New York: Columbia University Press. (Original work published in year unknown).

Buffett, Warren (2008). *Berkshire Hathaway Annual Report*. Retrieved from http://www.berkshirehathaway.com/2008ar/2008ar.pdf

Carnegie, Andrew (1920, 1888). *The Autobiography of Andrew Carnegie and his essay The Gospel of Wealth.* (2006 ed). Signet Publishing.

Cicero (1777). *Cato Maior de Senectute* (William Melmoth, Trans.). London. (Original work 44 BC).

Clements, Jonathan (2009). *The Little Book of Main Street Money: 21 Simple Truths that Help Real People Make Real Money.* John Wiley & Sons.

Costello, Dr R. and Miskall, Dr Edward W. (1934). *Autopsy Charles (Pretty Boy) Floyd.* (performed by E.R. Sturgis, Coroner). Columbia County, Ohio.

Galbraith, John Kenneth (1929). *The Great Crash* (1961 ed.) Pelican.

Getty, J. Paul (1976). *As I See It* (2003 ed). Los Angeles: The J. Paul Getty Museum.

Graham, Benjamin and Dodd, Graham (1934). *Security Analysis* (1940 ed.) New York: McGraw-Hill Publishing.

Hearn, Lafcadio (1897). *Gleanings in Buddha Fields.* New York: The Riverside Press.

Hill, Napoleon (1928). *The Law of Success.* Meriden, Connecticut: The Ralston University Press.

Hunter, George W. (1914). *A Civic Biology.* American Book Company.

John Templeton Foundation (2008). *Life Story.* Retrieved from http://www.templeton.org/sir-john-templeton/life-story

Kuo, Louise, and Kuo, Yuan-Hsi (1976). *Chinese Folk Tales.* Millbrae CA: Celestial Arts.

Lacey, Robert (1983). *Aristocrats.* London, England: Hutchison & Co. (Publishers) Ltd. and the British Broadcasting Corporation.

Loeb, Gerald M. (1965). *The Battle for Investment Survival.* (2007 ed.) John Wiley & Sons.

Mayer, Fanny Hagin (Ed. and Trans.). (1985). *Ancient Tales in Modern Japan: An anthology of Japanese Folk Tales.* Indiana University Press.

Nitobe, Inazo (1905). *Bushido: The Soul of Japan.* New York: The Knickerbocker Press.

Renehan, Edward J Jr. (2005). *Dark Genius of Wall Street: The Misunderstood Life of Jay Gould, King of the Robber Barons.* New York NY: Basic Books

Schwed, Fred Jr. (1940). *Where Are the Customers' Yachts? or A Good Hard Look at Wall Street* (1995 ed) John Wiley & Sons.

Sinclair, Robert S. (1984). *Thinking and Writing: Cognitive Science and Intelligence Analysis.* Washington DC: Center for the Study of Intelligence.

Standiford, Les (2005). *Meet You in Hell: Andrew Carnegie, Henry Clay Frick, and the Bitter Partnership That Transformed America.* Crown Publishing.

Templeton, John Marks (1987). *The Templeton Plan: 21 Steps to Success and Happiness* (James Ellison, Writer & Editor). San Francisco: Harper and Row Publishers.

Tyler, Royall (Ed. and Trans.). (1989). *Japanese Tales.* Pantheon Press.

Vaknin, Sam (2007). *Malignant Self Love: Narcissism Revisited.* Prague & Skopje: Narcissus Publications.

White, Bouck (1910). *The Book of Daniel Drew.* (1965 ed.) Larchmont NY: American Research Council

The Intelligent Investor's Mind

"Live, if you believe me now.
Wait not for tomorrow, for this time
will not come again:
Gather from today the roses of life."

Pierre de Ronsard, 1587